SECRET
COVENTRY

David McGrory

AMBERLEY

Acknowledgements

Many thanks to various people for their help including photographs, Rob Orland (see www.historiccoventry.co.uk), John Ashby, Margaret Rylatt, Craig Taylor, Jake Clarke, Danny Robinson, Lucinda Mongor, Coventry History Centre and its staff, the Herbert, Portable Antiquities Scheme, Coventry City Council and the British Library.

First published 2015

Amberley Publishing
The Hill, Stroud
Gloucestershire, GL5 4EP

www.amberley-books.com

Copyright © David McGrory, 2015

The right of David McGrory to be identified as the Author of this work has been asserted in accordance with the Copyrights, Designs and Patents Act 1988.

ISBN 978 1 4456 4709 8 (print)
ISBN 978 1 4456 4710 4 (ebook)

British Library Cataloguing in Publication Data.
A catalogue record for this book is available from the British Library.

Typesetting by Amberley Publishing.
Printed in Great Britain.

Contents

Introduction

This book goes where others haven't gone before, into prehistory and Roman times, proving Coventry really did have life before Leofric and Godiva. Amazing new and old finds are discussed within these pages showing that Coventry's ancient history is becoming more accepted and the chances of finding something important is really out there. Here we also look at many aspects of secret Coventry, the cult of Henry VI and the part the *Coventry Tapestry* plays. Talking of plays, we also look at the matter of William Shakespeare visiting and performing Coventry. We also look at some of Coventry's many lost buildings, some of which could have been saved. We look underneath Coventry at vaults, cellars, crypts and tunnels and some great pieces of ancient art hidden from sight. There's still a lot to be said about *Secret Coventry* but some of it isn't a secret anymore.

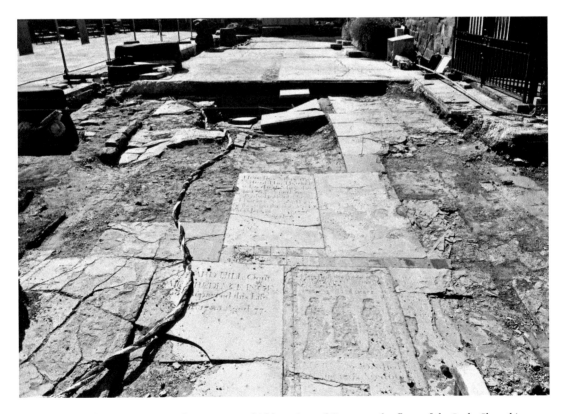

Uncovered in the summer of 2015 a secret hidden piece of Coventry the floor of the Lady Chapel in St Michael's unseen since the nineteenth century. It includes the grave of Elizabeth Lapworth who died in 1722 (front/centre) aged 100.

1. Hippos and Ancient Coventry

The land, which is now Coventry, has an ancient history going back to the age of dinosaurs and beyond. An example of its later history was reported on 4 February 1927 when we are informed:

> the skull of a hippopotamus extinct so far as Europe is concerned has been unearthed in Coventry. Workmen excavating the London and Midland Railway Company's ground at Coundon Road found the skull 15 feet below the surface. After extracting teeth as souvenirs the workmen threw it to one side. It was noticed by a local naturalist and taken for examination. The strata in which the discovery was made is of the red drift of the Pleistocene period, when Britain was part of the continent; the skull has been placed with the Coventry City Guild museum.

The skull was donated to the museum by naturalist J. H. Edwards and was thought to be at least 80,000 years old. Its preservation suggested that it died in the vicinity it was found and not carried in by later glacial deposits. Its body could have been washed away in the gravels or may still lie there.

This skull has caused controversy recently because of its condition. It has even been suggested that maybe it belonged to an animal that died with a travelling menagerie in the nineteenth century. Apart from the fact that all such shows were held in the city centre, mainly on Greyfriar's Green, there is no actual evidence that any hippo, a massively rare animal, has actually ever died in Coventry. The first hippo was brought to England in 1850 and its death was felt so significant that it was reported in the press in 1878. Wombwell's Menagerie had a hippo among its animals exhibited at Coventry Fair in 1852 and 1853 on Greyfriar's Green and it never died. In fact no one would bury a hippo when its skull or whole skeleton would be considered a major paying exhibit. Interestingly, a stuffed one stopped off in the city on its way to Birmingham in 1834 and caused quite a stir.

The finding of a hippo skull is far from impossible. Coventry in the Pleistocene was a temperate clime, a slightly green Africa and home to straight tusked elephants, hippos, rhinoceros and hyena to name a few. Through the area ran the massive River Bytham, which distributed gravels across the area, some of which are still excavated today. I think the fact that the animal's remains were found at the depth of fifteen feet in drift of the Pleistocene period says it all. In fact hippo teeth have been found at Baginton.

In later periods, there has been speculation some have thought the city had some form of inhabitation in the Bronze Age, others ridicule this. So where's the evidence? The idea that there could have been an ancient settlement in the centre of Coventry is, by experts, thought highly likely; in fact the Coventry Historic Landscape Characterisation Report by archaeologists for English Heritage and Coventry City Council in 2013 states:

Historically much of the research and archaeological investigation undertaken in the city has focused on the Medieval period but recent and ongoing archaeological work is demonstrating that there was significant prehistoric and Roman activity in the Coventry area. Mesolithic/Neolithic flint scatters have recently been recorded in the northwest of the city, where the rural landscape has enabled systematic field walking to be carried out ... It is therefore no surprise that occupation evidence from this period has also been found in Coventry ... The Roman period in Coventry is represented by occupation evidence in the vicinity of the eastern bypass and the city centre as well as a recently discovered settlement in the Upper Eastern Green area ... Current archaeological evidence puts the majority of Prehistoric and Roman sites around the periphery of the city but this is largely because these areas have received more attention in terms of archaeological fieldwork due to their rural character. Elsewhere the majority of land within the city is built up and early sites are more difficult to identify. It is therefore reasonable to suppose that other sites may exist across the city

This says it all. Coventry has an ancient history but in the centre it's harder to find. Evidence from the central area of ancient occupation certainly exists. One piece is mentioned by historian Spectator in the *Coventry Standard* on 20 March 1914. It says Hillfields had prehistoric lychets, farmed strips on the hillside.

Surely you remember, Mr Spectator that the hills at the back of Primrose Hill House, part of which is built upon and part of which forms a park, were terraced in the way you describe. Things which have been done to the hills in late years have left scarcely a trace of their former appearance'. The writer mentions the Giant's Grave, a tumulus crowned with ancient elm trees, 'which now lies buried beneath somebody's backyard – that it may have contained, not the bones of a giant, but remnants of the former civilisation which accompaniment the method of cultivation which the hillsides disclosed.

Another letter from that year says,

Across the first field, almost in direct line from Primrose Hill House, was a groove in the land, which might possibly have been one of the covered ways ... it seemed to have taken originally a direct course from the tumulus in Primrose Hill field ... It was just beyond this tumulus, near Stoke, that the rude pavement was found forty years ago. Also, at the north end of the field, lying nearest the brook, to the east side of it, was a peculiarly-shaped, shelving bank, obviously not a natural feature, but pointing to a 'previous occupation ...

In the *Coventry Standard* of March 1917 we find a description of the tumulus and where it stood. It says:

If you walk through the passage which leads from St Peter's Vicarage to Nicholls Street you will see a deep declivity, protected by a wall and palisades placed alternately, and just below where the wall ends and the houses begin there the tumulus was. The bandstand in

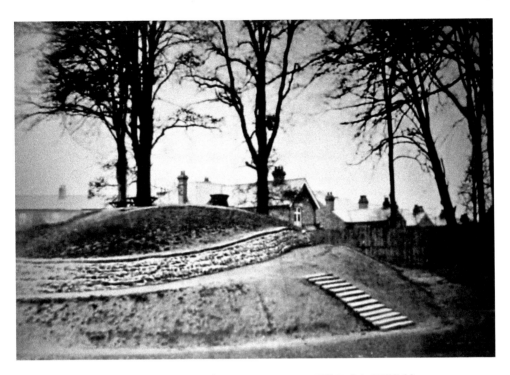

The Giant's Grave sitting on high ground in 1900 in Primrose Hill Park in Hillfields.

Primrose Hill Park is only a few yards away from the site of it. It was oblong, and in shape not unlike half an egg; there is a long tumulus in Uley, in Gloucestershire, much like it. It stood six or eight feet high, and was known as 'The Giant's Grave.' Thereupon it grew several full-sized elm trees ... When the neighbourhood took its present character a great deal of ground had to be made up for the west side of Nicholls Street, and the trees were felled, and the tumulus now lies buried beneath the hundreds of loads of soil which are the foundation of the back gardens of the houses erected close by ... Nor have I ever heard that any attempt was made to probe its mysteries. It was a remarkable thing to let this tumulus be lost in this way, because there were evidences all about of an unusual character.

In March 1917 Dr Wyatt Wingrave wrote of more mounds on Whitley Common, stating,

one which I can well remember, is not far from Charles' Mound, about 200 yards from the gate on the road leading to Baginton, where other mounds occur. This bears out my own supposition that there were other mounds in the park and the locality; the Mound is only separated from Whitley Common by a stone's throw. And we have evidence of the fact that the Mayor and certain of his brethren were summoned to London to answer for the conduct of the citizens in breaking into the mounds in the park.

Obviously the people of Coventry thought these mounds to be ancient and dug them for treasure. It was also believed in the past that there was evidence of a hill fort by

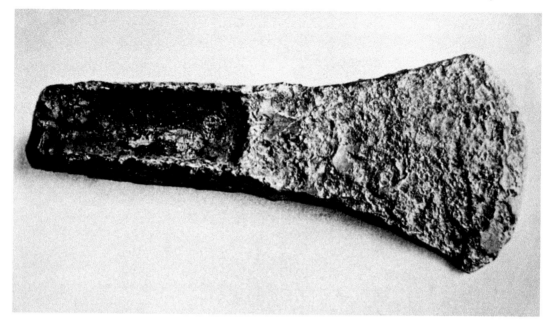

The Whitley axe found in an area of a prehistoric settlement.

Whitley Common with ditches and hollow ways. In 1928 a Bronze Age axe dating from 1500 BC was unearthed 500 yards from the chapel at Whitley Abbey, this was followed in 1932, a flanged Bronze Age axe head was found on the site of the present Jaguar Land Rover centre. The area beyond this site is now being developed, so any future discoveries may be lost.

In Cheylesmore Park once stood a large mound in the 'Mound Field', called 'The Mount'. It gets a mention in the *Coventry Standard* of 23 March 1917 when Spectator wrote:

> We understand that the agents of Lord Cheylesmore have obtained possession of some further land on the Coventry Park estate, which will be forthwith cut into small allotments for the purpose of growing food stuffs in the present crisis ... The Mound is not a very pronounced eminence, and will not offer any impediment to the gardener whose lot it shall be to cultivate it. When I went there the field was already scored into allotments, the little red trenches threading their way over the hill in vivid distinction, the deep green of the old turf, and plot was half dug just where the rise of the Mound began the north-west side ... Some historians say that the Mound was raised in 1627 – nearly three hundred years ago – and that an elm tree was planted in the middle of it ...

It continues:

> The great elm tree – the last survivor of the avenue, if ever an avenue there were – was blown down in a gale Sunday 24 March 1895, exactly twenty-two years ago ... It had long shown signs of decay, and when the first Lord Cheylesmore – then Mr H. W. Eaton – purchased

the Park he did what was possible to preserve it, putting new soil at its roots and binding it about with chains and clamps. But the great wind was too much for its endurance, and it fell like the giant it was. History states explicitly that the Mound was raised in 1627, but some antiquaries have held the opinion that though this may have been the year when the tree was planted upon it, the Mound itself is of far older origin – that it may, indeed, be an ancient tumulus. There were several tumuli in the vicinity of Coventry; the most pronounced was one in Primrose Hill Field, which has been buried in the development of the neighbourhood, and undoubtedly there were others, besides the one in the Park, traces of which have been lost ... In some places they are yet called Giants' Graves ... and many a legend attaches to them, and mysterious things are alleged to have followed the disturbance of them. Sometimes they have been regarded as the hiding places of treasure, and this idea has led to extensive vandalism and the destruction of innumerable grave mounds. There is evidence that the Mounds in our own Park suffered in this way, for the historians tell that the Mayor of this city and two Aldermen were summoned before the Council at London with respect to an attempt by the inhabitants to destroy mounds in the Park ... permission should be obtained off Lord Cheylesmore for the Mound to be

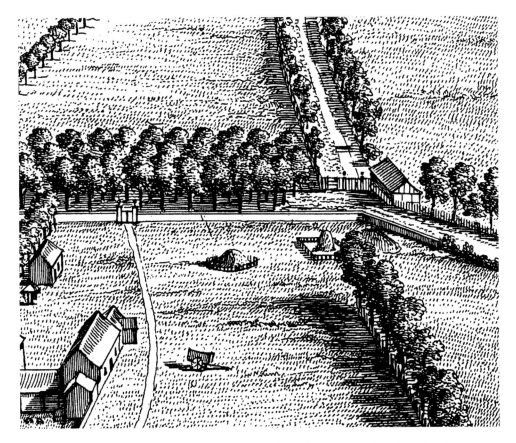

An engraving from 1729 showing a burial mound and standing stone at Coombe Abbey. There were a number of burial mounds spread over the estate and prehistoric and Roman settlement.

opened, to discover whether it really is a burial place, or whether it is simply an artificial mound, thrown up as a planting place for the last tree of that traditional avenue.

The mound sadly was never excavated and is now lost.

Barr's Hill was discussed by Spectator in June 1915; he writes:

I do not know who made Middleborough Road [it was laid out by Charles Bray, friend of George Eliot] ... The Middleborough Close was a well-wooded stretch of land, leading up from the Naul's Mill and Abbott's Lane to Barr's Hill and the Radford Road. It was marked by some ancient features. It is not at all impossible that Barr's Hill may have been a military camp ... Alderman Andrews once told me that there ran down the centre of it, just behind the line of houses on the north side, an ancient covered way, leading from the hill to the stream – one of those sunken roads by means of which the soldiers evaded the enemy while about necessary tasks ... This trench was undoubtedly filled in partly during the making of the street, for quite recently a number of curious objects were found during excavations there ...

What these objects were is sadly not recorded.

A correspondent to Spectator in July states:

Only the other day I heard the story of discoveries of a peculiar nature which were made on the north side of Middleborough Road ... Works of levelling were being done between the garden of one of the houses and the field beyond, and the excavations revealed the presence

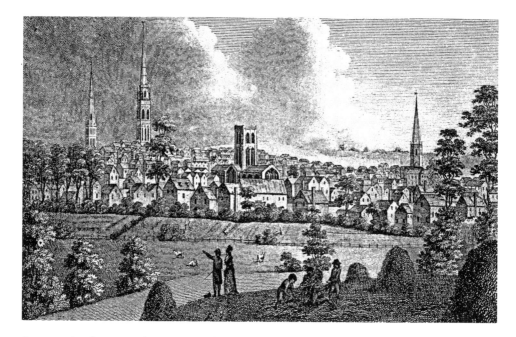

An engraving from 1794 showing part of the high ground that made up Barr's Hill.

of a considerable store of horns and bones ... The place of the burial, I have been told, bore traces of having been a passage of some kind in past ages ... a covered way formerly ran from Barr's Hill down to Radford Brook, a sunken V-shaped passage, by which soldiers in the camp on the brow of the hill could go unseen by the enemy to fetch water.

Interestingly, Barr is an ancient British word for hill top and can be found on hills in other places such as Oxfordshire. The word borough we find here, as in Middleborough, is an ancient word for a fortified place, which implies an ancient fortified place often possessing a tumulus or burial place. Barr's Hill had a small outwork dug on it during the Civil War, between the original Radford Road (St Columba's Close) and St Nicholas Street, with a sunken track connecting it to city (not the brook); this was quickly, however, found to be impractical and filled in to stop the enemy using it. This has been used in the past to explain the earthworks but of course is incorrect as this small outwork would have to have stood between two roads and wasn't even in the right area.

It was said that parts of the hill on the south and west side had remains of large ditches and terracing. The presence of large numbers of cattle skulls and bones are not likely on a small Civil War outwork, but common near prehistoric hill forts. Also it has been suggested that no remains of these ancient earthworks were found during the laying of the modern extension of the Radford Road in the 1960s. Apart from the fact that no decent watch was kept on the area, and literally mountains of earth were moved; most wasn't in the area mentioned in the early references to terracing and ditches.

The *New & Complete British Traveller* published in 1784 states, 'The site of an old town is supposed to have been on the north side of the present, not only because great foundations are discovered about the spot, called St Nicholas Churchyard, but we may add from the tumulus near it on the Atherstone Road [Radford Road] ...' Interestingly aerial photographs show the remains of two circular mounds on the Lydgate Road side of Barr's Hill.

The area from Gibbet Hill including Warwick University down to Earlsdon had significant occupation in prehistory. J. A. Wright while field walking, in a ploughed field by Gibbet Hill, in 1935 found a very significant find; an axe made at the great Neolithic/ Bronze Age axe factory in Graig Llwyd in Wales. Very few of these are found outside that area, and the area around Gibbet Hill has now yielded four; more than anywhere else outside of Wales. It was once thought that these finds suggested a trade route through the area, but now they are thought to simply reflect the large population in this area during the Mesolithic and Neolithic periods. In 1999 a watching brief was put on earthworks in the Riddings, Earlsdon and Iron Age objects were found. During work on an all weather pitch for the university, Iron Age roundhouses were discovered. Digging ended in 2002 and the press reported seventeen roundhouses had been discovered dating between 100 BC and AD 100. Dr Stephen Hill, one of the leaders of the dig, estimated many more on site; it is said up to 200, making it bigger than the Iron Age settlement at Maiden Castle. This would make it one of the largest Iron Age settlements in the country, not bad for an area which had previously been thought to have just casual losses by travellers. It seems most of these buildings were burnt. An interesting and likely true

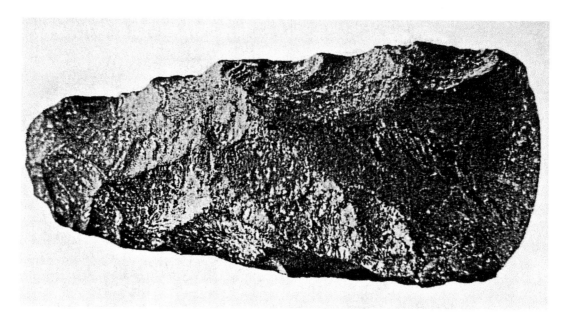

A Graig Llwyd axe found near Gibbet Hill, one of the first signs of a large prehistoric population in the area.

theory about the ending of the site was put forward by Margaret Rylatt suggesting that it had suffered Roman burnt earth policy after the Boudican Revolt. There is evidence of Roman occupation afterwards including a Roman road and villa in the area. This area has produced a number of gold and silver staters over the years.

Evidence of more ancient Mesolithic (10,000–4,000 BC) settlements can be found west of Fivefield Road in Keresley. In one field alone ninety worked flints have been discovered. This site lasted into the Neolithic period (4,000–2,200 BC); a second site lies a short distance away between Bennett's Road South and Tamworth Road. Other Neolithic sites have been found along the Tamworth Road and to the north at Upper Eastern Green. Interestingly, once north of Penny Park Lane (itself an ancient name from Peny-y-Parc) was Keresleyeberwe castel (Keresley Barrow Castle), the site of a large prehistoric barrow or defended enclosure. Mesolithic and Neolithic finds have been found from Corley camp, Hounds Hill down to Springfield Hill in Keresley. Fields in the upper area show lineal lines and a possible high-status banjo enclosure site suggesting more intense inhabitation.

A roughly carved stone battle axe of the late Neolithic to early Bronze Age was found in a garden in Green Lane. In 1948 a flint hand axe was found in gravels of the Sowe by Coventry Golf course. Off Unicorn Avenue, near Broad Lane, in 1968 a stone axe from Penzance was picked up on a building site by a stream. Also in the same year a stone axe-hammer was found in a garden in Greendale Road. At Westwood and Toll Bar Island by the Post Office Sorting depot Iron Age settlements have come to light. Both date from around the first century BC. Pottery and flint and a rare crucible for smelting metal have been found. The post office site also brought to light pot boilers (stones for cooking) and a chariot lynch pin; showing high status and an ancient wheeled vehicle in Coventry.

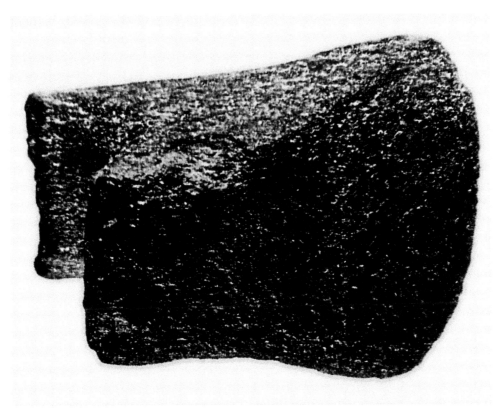

The 9,000-year-old Green Lane stone battle axe, a crude heavy weapon; the rear section is missing.

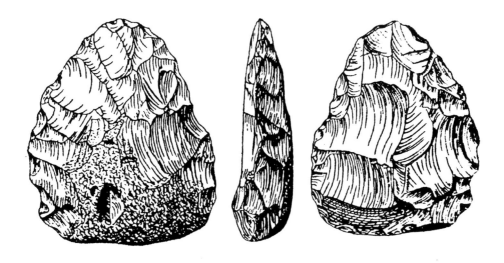

A fine flint axe found by the golf course in Hearsall.

Objects have also been found nearer to the city centre. Flint tools have been found at Charterhouse. In 1919 a partially ground flint axe was found in nearby Pinley. Around the same time a flanged Bronze Age axe was found between Spencer Road and Asthill Grove; part of a similar axe was also found in Allesley. A Neolithic barbed flint arrowhead was found in a garden in Wycliffe Road dating between 2,500 BC and 1,500 BC. I personally found a Neolithic flint scraper and hammer stone in my own garden dating to about 3,000 BC. A Neolithic axe hammer was found in a garden in Greyfriar's Road and a similar axe found near Whoberley Avenue. In a garden in Thistley Fields East, near Radford Road, a gold Gallo-Belgic stater was dug up in 1966, and a short distance away a Gallo-Belgic gold stater was found in Beake Avenue, Radford. The coin dated between 57 and 45 BC. Another important find reported in *West Midlands Archaeology* (35, 1992), by a metal detectorist in the Coundon area, was the end link of a decorative bronze bridle bit dating from the late first century BC to the early first century AD. This shows more Bronze Age high-status horsemen or chariots in the area.

Few wooden objects from this period survive except in mud, and John Bailey Shelton wrote of digging on the Rex Cinema site in June 1937, saying it was:

Once part of the extensive Bablake, and from its depth, varying from 10 to 14 feet, I hoped to find a tree trunk boat, early British, as three years ago, about 20 yards from this

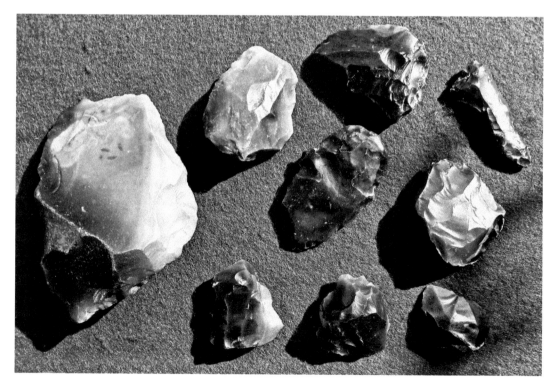

Worked flints from the Mesolithic to Neolithic period found in and around Coventry. The Neolithic scraper bottom right came out of my own garden!

site, I discovered a boat paddle of this period at 16 feet, and about 40 yards from here we discovered a wood ford, or bridge, which is thought to be Roman.

Interestingly, when Woolworth's was being built in the late 1950s hundreds of oak piles were found sticking out of the old lake bed. This area lay undeveloped before the early 1800s, suggesting that these piles were of ancient origin and may possibly suggest a causeway or lake village.

There are three other objects found within Coventry, which may have Celtic/Bronze Age/Iron Age origins; one is a stone carving of a head, which looks typically Celtic. This lies within Holy Trinity Church. The second object, another archaic looking stone head that was found in Willenhall, is now lost. The third, which is of unknown origin and has never been truly dated, is Coventry's Knave Post. This black oak figure was used as a whipping post, but its origins are unknown. It has been suggested it began life as a piece of church art but this is unlikely as it is very crude. It has also been said that the figure wears shackles; in reality these cannot be seen. I have a suggestion for the origins of this figure; there have across northern Europe been unearthed coarse wooden figures from

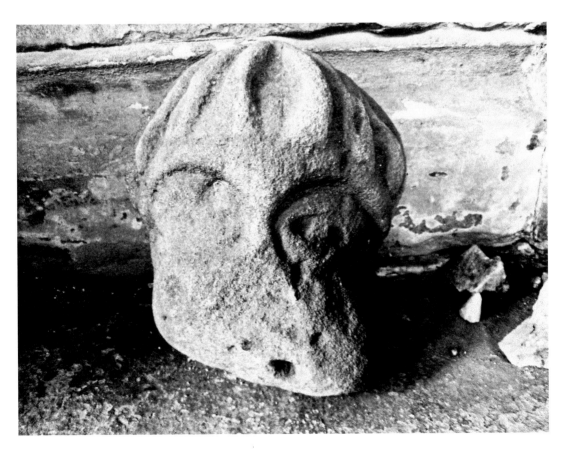

A sandstone archaic head in Holy Trinity Church. This was probably dug up in the churchyard in the past and taken within the building.

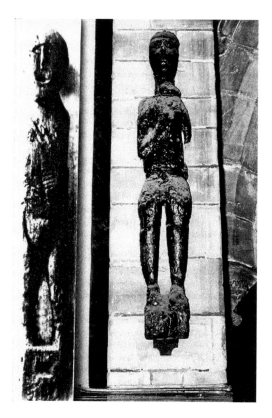

A bog oak deity dug up in Scotland and Coventry's Knaves Post. The similarity is remarkable!

the Celtic period. These are thought to be of unknown deities, which may have stood within tree groves. The surviving figures have all been unearthed in boggy ground or old lake beds, two conditions which could be found in Coventry. What do these figures look like? They look exactly like the knaves post, with the exception that some of the Knaves Post was recut in the nineteenth century. Some wear a torc around their necks, on the Coventry figure such a remnant can be seen, and they stand on block bases as does the Knaves Post.

Another forgotten artefact was rediscovered by myself while researching. While looking through photographs of the rebuilding of Broadgate in 1947 I noticed a typed piece of text on the back of a photograph of a digger in a large hole in Broadgate. It stated that while waiting for the digger to arrive a workman using a spade unearthed a Bronze Age axe head. With further research I discovered a photograph of a small display set up of the Broadgate finds by John Bailey Shelton.

The photograph showed many items from medieval times and among them the coracle paddle and the axe, a socketed and looped palstave dating from between 650 and 850 BC. This axe head, which was found within a few feet of the present-day statue of Lady Godiva, survives in the Coventry Collection and can be identified by a chip in its edge. There was, however, a second axe head of the same type found in a field at Canley among spoil dumped from Broadgate during the same excavations. Where this axe is I don't know but the axe found in Broadgate has been questioned, and as late as the 1960s dismissed, in case

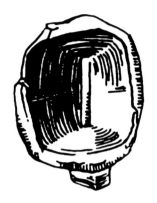
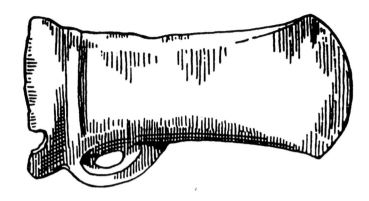

The Bronze Age Broadgate axe, this has in the past been confused with the one found shortly after in the spoil in Canley. This is, however, the axe that Shelton exhibited with other items shortly after it was found.

it was an unrecorded axe head from elsewhere; from a 'former museum, bombed during the war, [which] stood near this area …' The museum being referred to was Shelton's Benedictine Museum which actually stood quite a distance away in Little Park Street and, importantly, wasn't actually blown up. Also importantly, the axe wasn't unearthed till 1947, so how could it have been blown up? Despite some people's difficulty in believing it, a Bronze Age axe head was actually dug up about 14 foot down in Broadgate with a spade, and a second came out with the digger and was dumped in Canley.

This of course makes the discovery of two Bronze Age axe heads in Broadgate even more important. One axe could be a casual loss, but two becomes unlikely. A founder's hoard of damaged implements for resmelting is also unlikely. That leaves the probability of a deliberate burial as an offering on a sacred hilltop, a practice not uncommon in the period we are dealing with. There was also a third Bronze Age axe head, which was unearthed in the centre of Coventry on the site of one of Coventry's Pageant houses.

During the building of the lower precinct, behind the site of the present New Look store, an early Bronze Age perforated stone axe was found. Interesting items have come to light a short distance away in the area between Queen Victoria Road and the Showcase Cinema. These include in 1999 an Iron Age copper stater (coin) of the Corieltauvi tribe; the tribe which occupied this area. This, importantly, was not the only find, for later two gold Iron Age staters, one of the Dubonni tribe from South Warwickshire, were found on the same site in the middle of modern Coventry.

I think the lesson to conclude from this is that Coventry and its surrounds have an ancient history going back to the Mesolithic period. Places like Baginton and Gibbet Hill were, in the early twentieth century, thought of as having no ancient history, then over time it all came to light. Archaeologists who had previously thought the Coventry area had little prehistoric inhabitation now know better and are finding more and more encroaching on the city centre and justifiably now understand that there is no reason why Coventry's centre was not also inhabited, especially as it was ideal for inhabitation as it had ranges of woodland and sloping high open ground going down to lakes, rivers and springs, a magnet for wildlife and for habitation. Perhaps one day, underneath all the concrete, our prehistoric past will truly re-emerge.

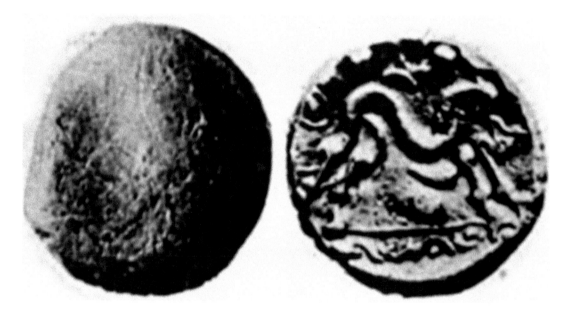

One of the gold staters found in the centre of Coventry.

2. Roman Coventry

On 21 August 1928 it was reported that a Roman site had been discovered five weeks previously within three miles of Broadgate. At this point the site was secret ... where was it ...? Baginton. Before 1928 it was thought the nearest Roman site to Coventry was in Kenilworth. This is a classic example of how history does not exist until it is discovered and much awaits discovery. As we have seen, ancient inhabitation around Coventry is greater than was previously perceived, but what of the Roman period? It has long been suspected that Roman roads cut through the area; one is thought to enter the city following part of the course of the present Foleshill Road or may cut across joining a secondary route following the route of the Stoney Stanton Road. In a field by the Foleshill Road in 1792 a large and very significant Roman find was made. It was reported in the *Coventry Mercury*:

On the 17 December last, was discovered in a meadow at Foleshill, belonging to Mr. Jos. Whiting of that place, in digging a trench, about two feet below the surface, an earthen pot, containing upwards of 1,800 Roman copper coins, principally of the Emperors Constantine, Constans, Constantius and Magentius; most of which remain in the possession of Mr Whiting, for the inspection of the curious. And on Sunday last, in continuing the same trench, he found another earthen jug, containing a greater quantity of larger coin; but the latter are in greater preservation.

On page 786 of the *Gentleman's Magazine* of 1793, a gentleman signing himself Explorator adds to the previous insert:

I send you a drawing of the pot in which the 1,800 Roman coins mentioned in your present volume, P.83, were contained; it was broken by the labourer, but the fragments have been cemented together, and the drawing is a faithful representation of its present appearance.

The second pot was much broken when discovered, but appears from the fragments to resemble the former, only is smaller; the coins though are said to be better preserved, and larger, were precisely the same sorts, &c., as those first discovered. I examined the coins found in the larger pot minutely, and was surprised to observe amongst that number only one scarce reverse, viz: CONSTANTINVS AUG.; reverse, SARMATA DEVICTA; of which being rather uncommon ...'

This intriguing hoard of nearly 4,000 coins, not 2,000 as often stated, was found at Bullester Fields farm between Foleshill Road and Stoney Stanton Road and adds weight to the evidence that an established Roman road or roads ran through the site of present-day Coventry. This hoard, like all hoards, must have been buried at an identifiable spot as the owner no doubt wished to return for it. This would be in an identifiable area near to a road, not in the middle of a heavily forested area, which would later become unidentifiable.

According to Roman finds a possible road entered the city from the north side. Barrs Hill, apart from having prehistoric association, also in the nineteenth century gave out Roman coins and pottery mirroring the dates of the Lunt Roman Fort. Early deeds refer to massive foundations on the site of St Nicholas' Church off the very top of St Nicholas Street, although these of course may belong to the church. There was also a Roman statuette found on the site in the early nineteenth century. A road may have entered the city via the present Bishop Street, going to the edge of the Babbu Lacu where fourteenth-century charters state massive ancient pillars stood and Shelton found a Roman quern and two hippo-sandals (Roman horseshoes) and a wooden causeway which once crossed the water. By this site of ancient pillars 'of great strength and size' (one survived into the nineteenth century and was of Roman design) was also unearthed in 1796 another now forgotten object; a Roman alabaster statuette of a warrior wearing a laurel crown. The figure was reported as being found 'considerably below the surface of Bishop Street and near to the Free School there'. With this and other finds we may have the answer as to why the track didn't bypass the centre as it may have some connection with the possible sacredness of the site and the fact that the Romans appear to have set up a shrine or shrines here.

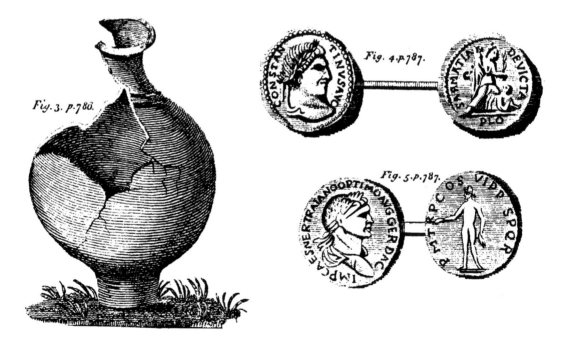

An illustration from the *Gentleman's Magazine* showing one of the pots and two of the coins in the Foleshill hoard.

Shrines. What's the evidence for that? Well, in May 1913 Mr T. S. Burbidge recorded the finding of a quantity of broken pottery of the Roman-British period, including part of a patera, in the Chapelfields district of Coventry and Alderman Andrews said that around the same time some Roman pottery was found in the Sherbourne. Interestingly a patera is a religious spoon or bowl used in making libations at a shrine. Talking of religion and shrines, there is a long-held tradition in Coventry that Roman general Agricola set up a camp on Barr's Hill and named the nearby settlement after the Romano-British water goddess, Coventina. One item found among the ruins of the old cathedral in 1856 adds weight to this rather unlikely tale. While workmen were at work on the site of the new Blue Coat School a medallion was found showing on one side a naked woman holding a flower and on the reverse the same naked woman pouring water from a jug. These are images used to depict Coventina. Interestingly also, for many centuries an ancient spoon, an actual patera, was kept in St Mary's hall and was called our Lady's Spoon.

If the idea of a Roman shrine in Coventry may seem, to those who think Coventry has no ancient past, unlikely. Well, in all probability there was one right in the middle of the city. Where? In Broadgate. A letter published in the Leamington Spa Courier of Saturday 8 July 1893 may enlighten us. It is written by J. A. Sparvel-Bayley a close friend of Matthew Bloxham, Warwickshire's most noted antiquarian of the nineteenth century, and it reads:

In the year 1792 there was discovered, near the Broad Gate, at Coventry, at a depth of nearly six feet, a very fine tessellated pavement, upon which was a 'middle brass coin' of the Emperor Nero. It is described as consisting of small coloured tessera arranged

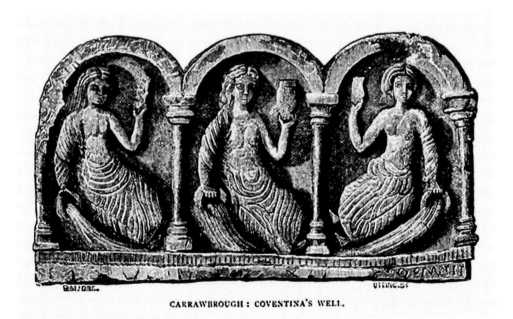

CARRAWBROUGH : COVENTINA'S WELL.

Part of a shrine to the goddess Coventina found in Yorkshire. The images mirror the medal found in Coventry.

in graceful design of scrolls and squares, with a labyrinth, the centre of which was unfortunately destroyed, but it had probably contained the figure of some deity. About the same time a small marble statuette, about ten inches high, was found in digging the foundations of a house in the old part of the town. The right hand is described as resting upon a shield, and the head was bound with a fillet resembling wheat. Although Coventry was certainly not occupied by the Romans for military purposes, it is quite evident from these 'finds' that they there enjoyed a domestic and tranquil existence. The private as well the public buildings of the Romans in Britain are known to have been abundantly ornamented with such pieces of emblematic statuary, and there can little doubt but that the figure found in 1792 represented one of the deities ...

When this important find was actually reported in the *Coventry Mercury* of 1792 it stated that a coin of the Emperor Nero had been found on a pavement in Broadgate. This remarkable piece of news was simply dismissed in the past because Coventry was thought to have no Roman past. It seems that the term pavement was in the eighteenth century a normal term for a mosaic, later however, in recent times, 'experts' didn't know this and dismissed this find because they assumed that the 'pavement' was a medieval slab pavement in the modern sense and the Roman coin sitting on it a misplaced find. As we can now see this is not so.

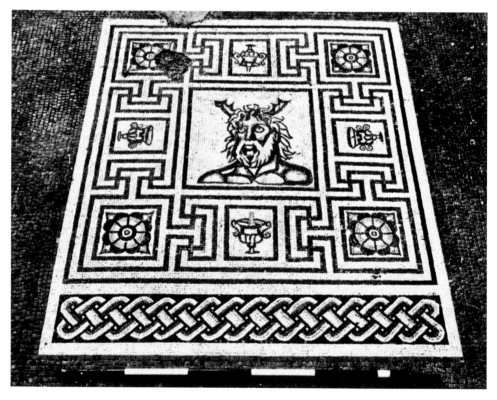

A similar mosaic to that discovered in Broadgate; this dates to the second century and bears the head of a sea god.

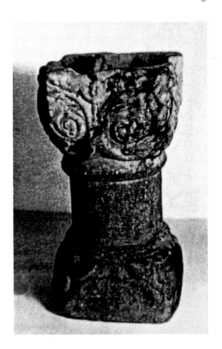

Possible Roman shrine lamp/burner found in Broadgate.

Interestingly Broadgate, as I said was the find spot of two Bronze Age axe heads which denoted probable ritual. Roman shrines were often built over earlier sacred sites and the fact that the centre of the mosaic was dug out does imply it bore the image of a deity as these were often dug out by people in search of votive offerings buried underneath. In 1928 when the ground was being excavated for Lloyds Bank in the High Street a very short distance away, a white stone lamp was found looking like a short column with naturalistic leaf designs. It now stands in the Herbert and was dated to the twelfth century and Romanesque, Norman. Anything in the past found in non-Roman Coventry tended to be assumed to be Norman ... Romanesque. Interestingly, this object made of a non-local stone matches the style of lamps used in Roman shrines. Back in the 1930s a large highly decorated column capital was found buried under the front of the Council house. This again was described as Romanesque but potentially could have been Roman. In nearby St Mary's Hall in the Armoury is an ancient partially recut worn carving. It shows a bearded god, like Neptune, with a leaf type crown; the same image of this deity can be found in Roman Britain. There is also a small Roman capital built into the wall of Holy Trinity's vestry.

Back to Broadgate, this remarkably is not the only mosaic to be found in 'non-Roman' Coventry, for in 1896 William Gutteridge, an artisan and collector, donated 'fragments of a Roman tessellated pavement' dug up near Warwick Lane to the proposed new Guild Museum which was to be set up in St Mary's Hall. It was reported in the *Coventry Herald*, 6 March 1868, 'on the site of the houses pulled down in 1820 are foundations of groined cellars, and still deeper, traces of an old pavement, said to be Roman, were discovered during the excavations for a sewer some years ago'. There's that word again, 'pavement', said to be Roman and below the medieval cellars. There is also another reference to a

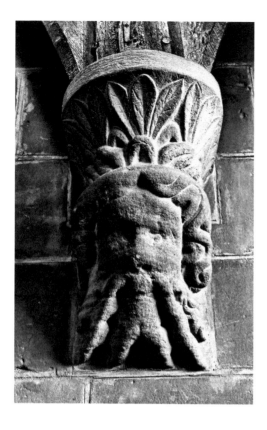

A probable Roman carving in St Mary's Hall.

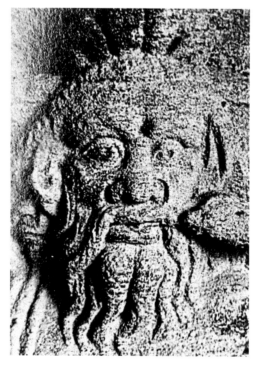

A second-century Romano-British water god; the likeness is unmissable.

Roman pavement being found behind Cross Cheaping in the late nineteenth century but no detail. More pieces of Roman tessellated mosaic were also unearthed in the centre of Coventry within the last forty years at digs led by archaeologists. Recently a builder told me of the many times in the past that they were told to rebury anything that could stop work in the city centre. He recalled one time digging up lots of small 'really old' coloured cubes in the centre of Coventry; he believed they were part of a Roman mosaic ... they were told to rebury them. Other builders have told of similar events. Roman mosaic does normally, of course, mean settlement and not just the odd Roman passing through. The statuette found in 1792 discovered by the Old Grammar School was a statue of the god Mars; the wheat sheaf denotes him in a dual role as god of agriculture and of war. So we have two Roman statuettes found on entering the city from the north.

Crossing Shelton's causeway over the lake an ancient trackway has been unearthed many times at the rear of and under the present Burges/Cross Cheaping area. In the nineteenth century on two occasions a track was unearthed behind the Burges, and Shelton uncovered the same stone track in the 1930s. Further up, in the mid-nineteenth century, workmen unearthed a third statuette, a 10-inch-high marble statue of Mars, while they were digging behind Cross Cheaping. This statuette, like the 1792 one, shows one of the legions' most favoured gods leaning against a shield, and this time holding a wheat sheaf, again in his dual role as god of war and of agriculture. The presence of such statues suggests marking the track up to the main shrine in Broadgate, maybe to the god Mars.

The coin of Nero was not the only Roman coin to be found on Broadgate Hill, for the nineteenth-century historian William Fretton wrote, 'I have several Roman coins found in this locality'. I myself have a coin of Domitian found in Broadgate during rebuilding in 1947, also Roman pottery. In the Municipal Exhibition in 1945 wooden water pipes, found in Broadgate and believed to be Roman, were exhibited. Were they connected to the shrine? A shrine ideally has a water source, and there was a large spring fed well in Broadgate. I also have an unsourced reference to Roman vessels being found in the Cross Cheaping/Broadgate area. In 1928 mention is made of a Roman urn found in the city centre. Numerous other things must have been found in the past and never recorded.

Small items that say much were found by Shelton's excavation in the Sherbourne in Cox Street in 1933. Here he brought to light, 'pottery, a coin of Galinus, AD 253–288, a bronze ring, a jet ring and a toilet set for nails and ears'. 'Who knows', he wrote, 'what may lie beneath the earth at no great distance from here.' The British Museum reported back on the finds that the objects were the contents of a Roman lady's satchel. Nathanial Troughton, who lived in Priory Row, made pencil drawings of a number of Roman items found in the Sherbourne in the mid-nineteenth century, but sadly they haven't survived. William Hickling states in 1846, 'There is also reason for supposing it [Coventry] to have been a town in the time of the Romans from the number of Roman coins and relics which have been found at various times in excavating in and about Coventry.' Sadly what these many Roman relics were we will never know.

In 1971 excavations on the Priory site unearthed a coin of Constantine from AD 305–06. In 1999 during excavations on the Priory only fourteen coins were found; one was Roman, another Constantine. Back in 1853 Edward Phillips of Coundon Hall exhibited a

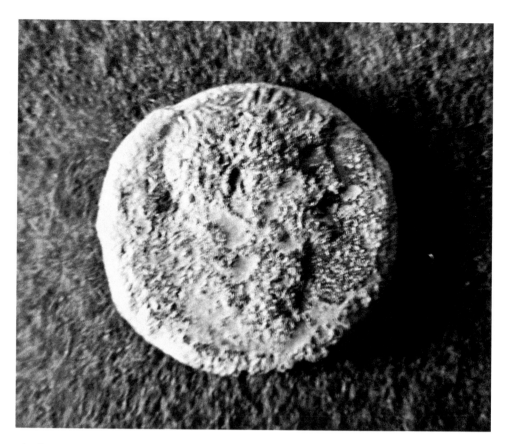

The first-century coin of Domitian found in Broadgate.

coin of Crispus found in the Sherbourne. Many more Roman coins have been found on top of and all around Broadgate Hill and all over the city centre. During a recent dig (1999) in Gosford Street a Roman fibulae brooch was unearthed. A third-century Roman coin probably of Constantius or Constantine was unearthed during excavations in Much Park Street in 1970–74. Around this area is also Jordan Well, a well associated with medieval mayor Jordan Sheppey. The well, however, is known to have existed before Sheppey's birth. Other Jordan Well's (and Jordan Hill's) around the country have been found to be of pagan, Celtic or Roman origin, associated with either well shrines or standing shrines. This is suggestive that Jordan is a corruption of the name of a deity.

Roman pottery was unearthed in Spon Street in 1976 and coins of such emperors as Antonius Pius, Gordian, Maxima, Julian and others have also been found in Keresley, Radford, Coundon, Whoberley and Stoke. In 1912 a Roman pot in coarse greyware from Wappenbury was unearthed in Broad Lane. In nearby Broomfield Road Roman pottery was discovered. More Roman pottery was found near Centaur Road. It is also worth pointing out that Shelton said he had 'a number of Roman objects' found in the city centre in his collection, most if not all of these are now lost. I, do however, have some second to third-century Wappenbury greyware dug up in Broadgate in the late 1940s.

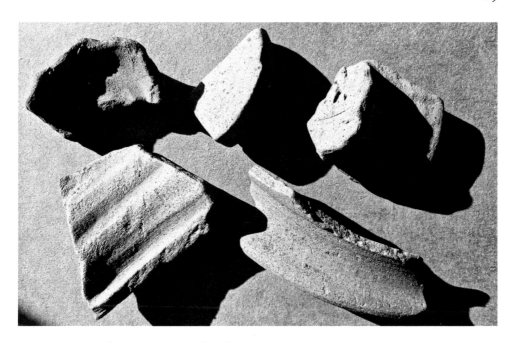

Roman grey ware from Wappenbury found in Broadgate.

In 2013 The Archaeological Data Service stated that:

There is also possible evidence for a Roman road at Cox Street, which is located *c*. 200 metres to the west of the study area. Excavations here in the early twentieth century uncovered a possible Roman river crossing for a putative road running from Mancetter to the north and Baginton to the south.

Another clue for possible lost Roman roads is mentioned in the *Coventry Standard* 23 May 1855. It says:

the workmen employed in making the cutting for the new street from Ford Street to East Street, when just at the brow the hill in the Swanswell fields, came upon a bed of broken stone, a foot or two below the surface, precisely similar to that used for macadamizing our turn-pike roads, though not quite of so flinty quality. Of this broken stone some loads have been dug out, and the vein of it is supposed to extend some distance out of the line of the cutting. There was also found a considerable quantity of other rough stone, in slabs of various sizes evidently not natural to the land.

In the *Coventry Standard*, March 1914, we have, 'when Raglan Street [in the 1830s] was being made there was regarded a remarkable occurrence, as it was supposed that it was part of a buried street was uncovered. The same thing occurred years afterwards, when the first plan was suggested of connecting Hillfields with Stoke. A street line was staked out from Kingston's Gate, from where Nicholls Street now is, across to Swan Lane in a northerly direction, and a few feet below the surface a section of pavement was found beneath the grass land'.

In reality Roman coins and pottery have been found in every district of Coventry. New Roman sites have been discovered in recent years in Eastern Green, a Roman settlement or villa near Willenhall Woods, where building material, pottery, including high-status Samian, were excavated dating from the second and third centuries. Coins, Samian pottery and loom weights have been found near Coombe Abbey. The list grows yearly.

Recently the Coventry Historic Landscape Characterisation Final Report, English Heritage Project no. 5927 stated of the city centre:

> Current evidence suggests that occupation during the Roman period was not prolific but recent fieldwork has found evidence of settlement immediately east of the Herbert Art Gallery and Museum in the city centre.

So, according to an official report we have Roman settlement in Coventry. This of course refers to the recent discovery of a Roman ditch, pottery and brooch between the Herbert and University buildings. This gently sloping ground leading down to the river is an area known by pollen tests to have been lightly wooded with birch and alder even in the Anglo-Saxon period and highly suitable for habitation. A full dig was not possible because of modern buildings and the fact that much of the archaeology, like elsewhere in the city, has been destroyed or is buried under concrete, leaving us with the odd finds which we had and still do have all over the city centre. A Roman coin was found on the University site near Cox Street recently. All this within a stone's throw from where Shelton found the Roman lady's make up tools. We may be on the brink of something special ... all it takes is a hole in the right place and the right person and Roman Coventry may burst into life, like the Lunt. It does appear that Roman Coventry is becoming more and more accepted. What I have told you is only a fragment of the city's secret ancient past. So, next time someone tells you Coventry had no Roman past, tell them it definitely does ... and that's official.

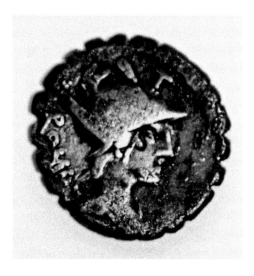

A silver serrate denarius of the Roman Republic dating to 80 BC found by John Ashby in Keresley.

3. Tunnels, Crypts and Hidden Chambers

All cities have stories of secret tunnels and Coventry is no exception. Old stories tell of tunnels, caves and caverns in the city. The priory undercrofts under Hill Top may have given rise to the stories of caves in the hillside, or they may have later been built into caves. One of the old tales of St George in the city suggests a dragon lived in a cave under Hill Top. Stories are told of tunnels everywhere. One of the most remarkable ones I recall was a lady told me when she was young in the 1920s her family lived in Much Park Street. One particular day her brother began to dig up the floor of their cellar; the ground collapsed under him and he fell about eight feet into a tunnel. This tunnel was investigated by local antiquarians and a number of ancient weapons were found. Apparently it went in the direction of Whitefriar's monastery. Old information suggests that it may have been a drain, probably connecting the rich merchant's houses with Whitefriar's drainage system. What became of it she could not recall but being so deep down it must still be there.

Up until the beginning of the twentieth century it was claimed that a secret passageway which ran from the Pilgrims Rest to the Priory could still be entered and that an ancient groined undercroft survived here. By 1917 it was said they were impenetrable. William Fretton said in 1879:

> Near the old gateway leading from Much Park-street to the White Friars, is a long vaulted apartment extending East and West with its entrance on the North side; it's not improbable, that as it stood near the outer gate of the monastery, it formed the basement story of the guest house attached to such an institution.

In the *Coventry Standard*, 5 November 1915, Spectator wrote:

> while walking back along Jordan Well it chanced that I again met the friend who had told me of the beam (an ancient beam from the Black Lion) ... Said he, 'Did you ever hear of the underground passage which runs beneath Gosford Street? It is supposed to have been a subterranean way between the White Friars Monastery and the exterior of the city in Mill Lane.' 'Oh,' I replied, 'that must be a piece of fancy, and deserves to be placed in the same category as the tradition which says there was underground way from Godiva's Priory to Kenilworth. You know all about that, of course.' 'Yes,' he said, 'but this is quite correct, for I myself once walked quite thirty yards along the passage I am speaking of.' That puts another aspect to the matter, I admitted 'and it would be interesting to know about it, for this is the first time I have heard it mentioned.' The following is what he then told me. I am speaking of a long while ago, in the fifties. The opening into the passage was in what used to be called the New Court, now No. 11 Court, in Gosford Street, just below the Mermaid ... The passage came from beneath the

houses, and apparently went right under the street, and it was possible to traverse it for a considerable distance. I have said, I once went under it for probably thirty yards. When one had walked a little way one came to a wall with an opening in it just wide enough to pass through, and on the other side of the wall the passage opened out again. A little further there was another narrow slit in an opposing wall, and then another opening out and that is as far as I went. The walls were stone, and the passage was vaulted.

Spectator recalled more:

One the alleged passageways was in the gardens in Mill Lane, which were occupied by Mr Jakeman, a well-known market gardener in those days. The city wall crossed Cox Street almost there, and you may remember that on the north side of what is now Godiva Street, at the Mill Lane end, some very old buildings stood until the street was made. These old houses ran back from the street into the gardens of Corpus Christi Lane to the cul-de-sac and at the far end of the row, near the river, and outside the line of the city wall, the end of the passage was to be seen. 'What was it like?' I asked, for that was worth listening to. 'There was flat stone,' said my friend, which was lifted by means of a chain, and I remember that when the stone was raised they used to fasten the end of the chain to a tree. In the opening thus revealed were several stone steps, leading

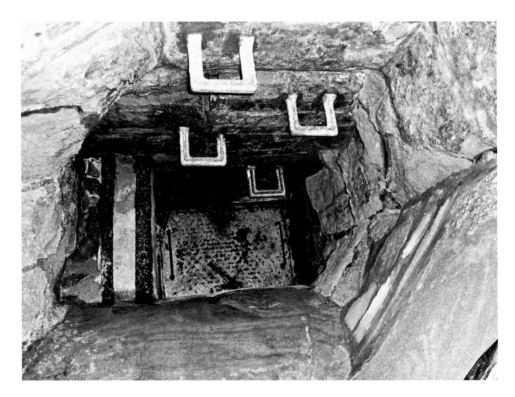

This narrow passageway with metal steps goes up into a city centre street. It does, however, lead down to a cellar. Such finds as this could leads to stories of secret tunnels.

down to the passage at the other end was supposed in the White Friars Monastery, as I have said, where the Workhouse now is, and it was thought that the passage was constructed to give the Friars the opportunity of leaving and entering the city for secret purposes, or when the city gates were shut. 'Nothing can be seen of it now,' he added. In answer to a further question a man fell into the opening in New Court and broke his leg, and it was then sealed to prevent further accidents. All the neighbourhood of Jakeman's Gardens has now changed, and probably Godiva Street runs over the place where the opening was …

In 1851 an underground stone passage seven feet square was found underneath the National School in Union Street. It appears to have been heading in the direction of Greyfriar's and it was suggested that it may have been a drain but it didn't appear to be heading for the river. It was said in the past that several large passageways had been unearthed in the vicinity of the Priory and one 'of very large dimensions' crossed Earl Street and under the Palace Yard. The idea of a tunnel running from the Priory to Kenilworth is an old one; dogs have said to have gone missing down both ends … the likelihood of its actual existence however, apart from being unlikely, doesn't actually make any sense. It has even been suggested that the story of a tunnel between Coventry and Kenilworth may date back to early medieval times when an order was given to cut the trees back on the Kenilworth Road to protect against robbers; it was like a wide tunnel.

One secret chamber that is hardly now a secret was mentioned in March 1876 by historian William George Fretton, who said that the late Dr Troughton, who lived in Priory Row, spent a great deal of time investigating its buried portions. He said:

he once pointed out to me a spot about half way down Hill Top (which crosses the site of the great transept and descends very rapidly from Priory Row to New Buildings), where, during the excavations made for the sewerage, the workmen came across the top of narrow pointed doorway, ten feet below the present surface of the roadway at that point … clearing away the debris, it was found to lead to a stair turret, the stairs descending: unfortunately it was not traced further, or discoveries of great interest and value might have been made. I have been informed by a late resident in Priory Row, that the passage was found in the lower portion of gardens, behind the house about thirty years ago, leading to chambers, the existence of which was not now known

This is particularly interesting for these steps and doorway were also unearthed during the dig in 1999/2000 and the secret underground chamber is now known as the Priory Undercroft of which tours are available.

The Spotted Dog, which was built on the site of the gatehouse of the priory on the site of the present Flying Standard pub, leading into the front court of the monastery, had groined cellaring, solid walling and two deeply splayed window openings. These cellars may have belonged under the gatehouse of the Priory. There are also cellars underneath present Lychgate Cottage, but these are barrel vaulted and made of later brickwork, not medieval.

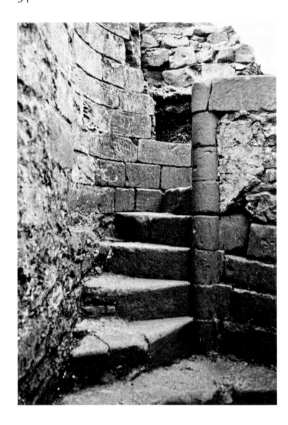

The steps that Dr Troughton first
discovered off Priory Row.

At the end of October 1968, a large cellar came to light to the right of the entrance to the
Council House. Interestingly, the cellars of all those houses that stood in Earl Street were
used to create the lower ground floor of the council house. On the other side of the road by
the shops small drain covers can be seen; these lead down into a large fourteenth-century
cellar under the present Civic Centre 2. The cellar has three entrances, including two from
the street; one has steps and slopes for moving objects and once had a door about ten
feet below road level. A quarter of this cellar is presently held up by blocks so it is hard to
appreciate its full size.

Recent work in the ruins of St Michael has helped to rediscover forgotten crypts; the
building has nine known ones. One on the east side was found to be filled, floor to ceiling,
with carved stonework when the building was being cleared of rubble. Under the inner
north aisle lies the lorry vault unknown until 1963 when a lorry delivering slabs into the
ruins fell into it. On the North side are two crypts, both accessible; the oldest of these,
measuring 38 feet by 23 feet, dates to about 1300 and lies beneath St Laurence's Chapel,
originally the chapel of Our Lady of the Mount which forms the Eastern extremity of
the North Aisle. Access was gained from a doorway and nine steps from the churchyard,
and the floor lies considerably below ground level. For many years this crypt was used a
burial place and had a number of lead coffins inside. At the time of the restoration of the
church in 1830 it was cleared out. The crypt adjoining it is divided into two by aisles with
octagonal pillars and the south corner is cut out of solid rock.

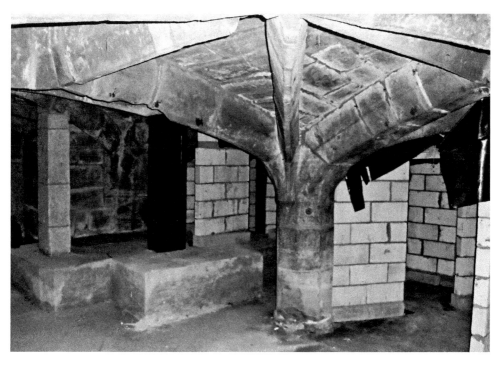

A few feet below Earl Street the cellar has nice columns and groining.

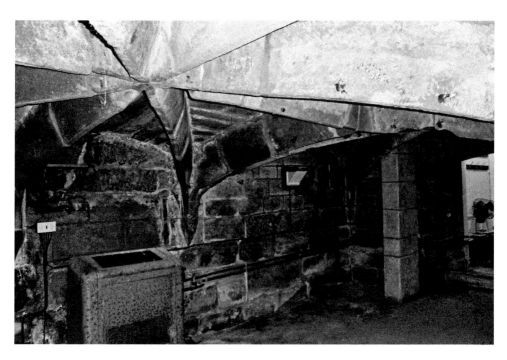

The groining is heavy to take the weight above it. This cellar has three access points including steps and a doorway from the street, now covered.

Adjoining this crypt on the eastern side is another of smaller dimensions; 22 feet 8 inches by 16 feet 6 inches. Evidently of more recent date, this crypt also had an entrance from the churchyard and used to communicate with the Drapers' or Lady Chapel above by means of a straight stone stair.

This crypt was probably used for mortuary services and later used as a charnel-house for storing bones. On the removal of the accumulated mass of bones in 1830 a piscina and altar were found, also a staircase which seemed to connect to another vault which at that time was hidden, probably under the present Lady Chapel. Interestingly, recent work around this area has shown that the actually church floor slopes downwards towards the east end; it was raised in 1830. In parts it is up to three feet deeper than the present level, but some of this may be due to the crypt below being partially collapsed. The original floor is also covered with tomb stones, mainly of drapers such as the Lapworths, Thackers, Hills and Inges. One stone is of Elizabeth Lapworth, who died in 1722 aged 100 years. My three-times great-grandparents, the Bradnicks, lie nearby in the Chancel; my three-times great-granddad John was churchwarden here for many years in the late eighteenth century. His daughter married Sir Skears Rew, twice mayor of Coventry; they lie in the Girdler's Chapel. Beneath the Girdler's there is another vault, at the moment inaccessible. There are also indications of a crypt having existed below the south chancel aisle and beneath the apse and part the choir. Scanners have also shown other vaults and unknown anomalies beneath the building.

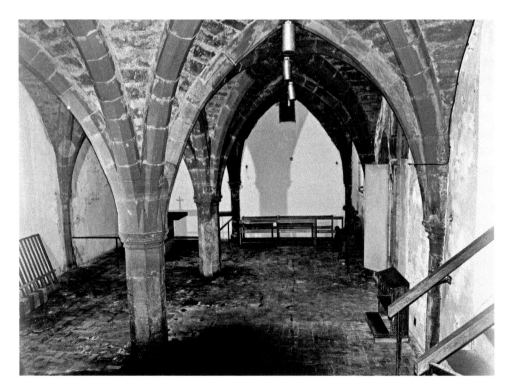

The multivaulted crypt of the Chapel of Unity underneath the old Cathedral.

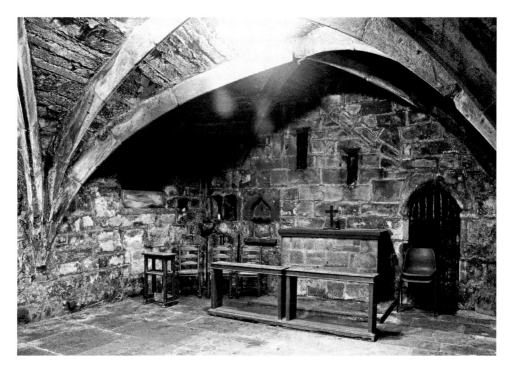

The Wyley Chapel beneath the ruins; note the piscina.

Under the north side of Trinity Church are a series of known crypts; the most notable of these lies under the Marler's Chapel and is one of the few full charnel houses in the country, still full of bones and skulls. This was originally entered by a covered entrance from the churchyard. This entrance was removed in 1695 and an opening was made in the floor of Marler's Chapel, but this was later closed off.

St Mary's Hall has the largest publicly accessible undercroft in the city. It consists of two chambers; the largest measures about 56 feet by 30 feet and is divided into two aisles by a row of octagonal pillars. The entrance opens into the courtyard and bears the mark of a master mason on the left. The undercroft was a storage space during the civil war; guns and powder were stored here, plus cannon and other weapons. Later it was found to be filled with rubbish up to six feet deep, and when this was cleared a well was found in the south-west corner. The smaller chamber, used by the Freemen, fronts the street and is about 30 feet long by about 12 feet wide; this is thought to have a hidden spring behind the west wall. The great hall upstairs extends the whole length above the two crypts. The smaller chamber is sometimes mentioned in old documents as the 'Tavern under St Mary Hall'.

Underneath what was Nos 21, 22 and 23 High Street, under the entrance to the Rose and Crown yard, now the yard of the Courtyard pub, may still be a large vault. It was noted in the past that although these cellars were divided into three, they were in fact originally one cellar entered through a central door and extending from east to west a massive 60 feet. The surviving part of this vault dating from the fourteenth century now lies under the Coventry Building Society.

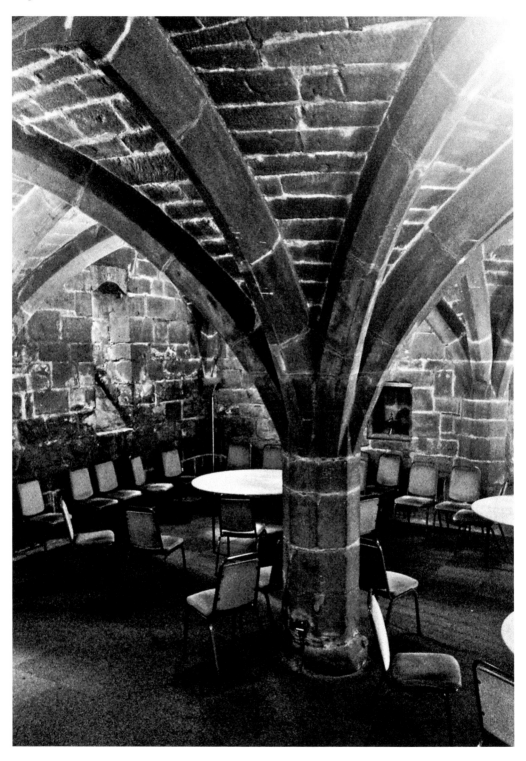

The fine vaulted undercroft under St Mary's Hall. This vault stored gunpowder and even small cannon in the fifteenth century.

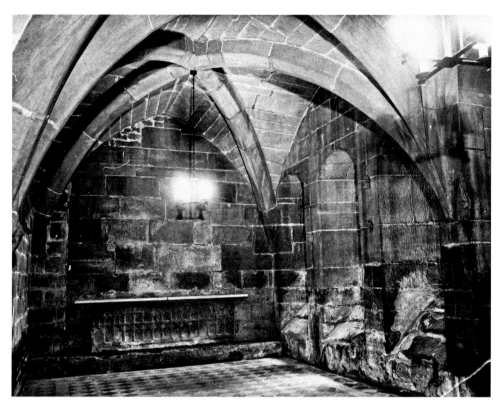

Above: The front cellar under the hall now used by the Freemen of the city.

Below: This image, created by Thomas Tickner in 1884, shows the cellar under the corner of Little Park Street. Is this still under the grass through the metal cover?

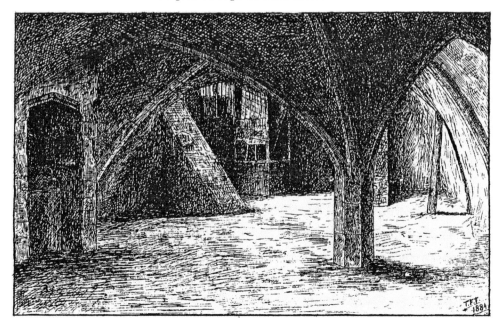

There was, and still may be, a curious cellar which lay under No. 51 Earl Street, which stood on the corner of Earl Street and Little Park Street, under the grass opposite the council house. The roof was formed of a quadruple series of vaultings, resting on a central octagonal pillar. The central column had ribs of varying lengths because the cellar was disproportioned, giving it a strange, confused appearance, a bit like a stone tree in a weirdly shaped room. It could of course still be there. In fact on the grass area here is a metal cover, which is said by council maintenance men to cover the entrance to a cellar which no one in modern times has entered or has a key for. Don't assume they were all filled in.

One of the best publicly accessible deep cellars in Coventry is under the corner of Bayley Lane. In the late nineteenth century this sat under Charles Woodcock's house. It is 22 feet by 11 feet 6 inches. It was approached from the house down a flight of stairs and down a passage on its western side, 14 feet in length. The house above was destroyed in the war and it now has an extended entrance from the Herbert.

Under the King's Head Hotel, which used to stand on and to the right of the Lady Godiva newsagent in Broadgate, were substantial vaults of considerable age. These vaults had an entrance which started wide then grew narrower as it went down. The last time these were used was in the war as an air raid shelter; the hotel was destroyed and presumably these ancient vaults were filled in. When alterations were made in Broadgate in 1821–22 on the west side, the houses were set further back. The cellars in some instances were not believed to have been entirely destroyed and are thought to still lie under present-day Broadgate. Under what was No. 58 Cross Cheaping was a kitchen in the cellar, and below it another cellar carved out of the solid rock. It was accessed through the floor of the room above, by a flight of stone steps and through a pointed doorway. Potentially this deep cellar, carved from the living rock, still exists, buried under modern Cross Cheaping. The area of Cross Cheaping and Ironmonger Row is particularly interesting, for beneath it is access into a huge hidden underground area which runs under Primark. This area began life as a large ancient quarry and was used to form the underground storage for the first Owen building built in 1936. It now forms a storage area for Primark.

Recently restoration work of the Old Grammar School should have revealed a hidden entrance, but none was noticed; there is however said to be a vault underneath it. In the press in the 1950s it was written, 'Parts of it are still visible to anyone interested by descending through the hole in the floor on the north side.' There was also said to be another cellar, below the library which previously straddled the area later known as Hales Street. This was described in the early twentieth century as still accessible, crossing under the road to the other side to what was then Hammon's Tailors. The person who recalled it said you could hear the vehicles rumbling above your head.

Whether most of Coventry's tunnels were drains we do not know, but most likely many were. That said, considering the dimensions of these drains, they certainly could be used for other purposes such as tunnels, to move about unseen, to escape, so perhaps they are secret tunnels. I assume there are still tunnels under the edges

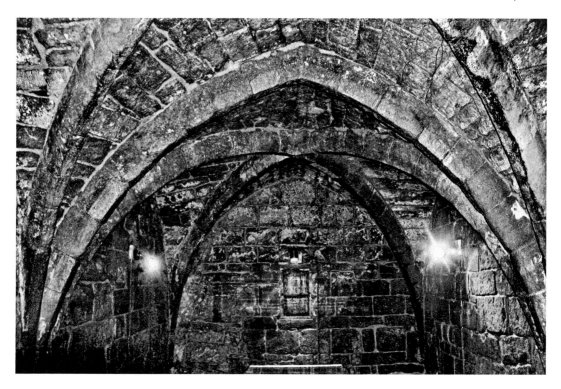

Above: The cellar below the frontage of the Herbert.

Below: An engraving by W. R. Groate showing the cellar which still exists under the High Street.

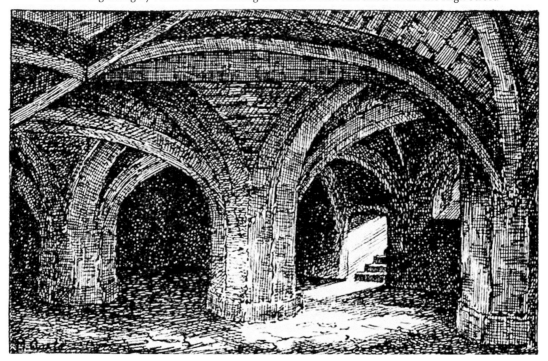

of Broadgate once known as the subways. Coventry's biggest, longest secret tunnel is of course still there, it's called the River Sherbourne. It disappears under the city just before Gosford Street, re-emerges for a few feet behind the Burges and goes off under the Burges, underneath the Lower Precinct at the bottom of the slope and re-emerges behind Ikea. This truly is a tunnel, a secret concrete tube running under the city, which few have ever seen.

4. Shakespeare and Players in Coventry

During the Elizabethan and Jacobean period Coventry was one of the main centres in England for drama. Many often ask if Shakespeare played Coventry; the answer to that is yes. Shakespeare was thought by some to be acting with the Queen's Men when they played the city every year from 1585 for six years. He was acting with the Chamberlain's Men in 1594 and his last time playing the city was in his thirty ninth year in 1603 when he appeared with the King's Men. When Shakespeare retired back to Stratford, no doubt he visited Coventry again.

Interestingly, Sir Thomas Lucy of Charlecote was the patron of a troupe of actors who played Coventry in 1584; a year before young Shakespeare is generally believed to have left Stratford when Lucy is supposed to have issued an arrest warrant on him for deer poaching. This is said to have been done on the Elizabethan table which now stands in the Old Council Chamber in St Mary's Hall. It has been suggested in the past that Shakespeare couldn't have poached deer as Charlecote had no standing herd. Writers have looked for other nearby herds such as Fulbrooke. This isn't necessary, for all country estates in England in this period had a population of wild deer. These wild deer belonged to the Lord of the Manor and it was an offence to take them. So there were always deer to poach, standing herds or not.

Shakespeare definitely played Coventry as a man, but did he visit the city in his youth? Well he certainly seems to have seen the Mystery Plays in the city. This can be seen by his numerous references to them. He must have seen them for he couldn't have read them, as they were not in print. Shakespeare's allusions to the plays must therefore come from his memory.

Here are some examples:

The boy in *Henry V* (IV. 4) compares Bardolph to the roaring devil in the old play, 'that everyone may pare his nails with a wooden dagger'. What old play? John Heywood (a contemporary of Shakespeare) tells us:

> For as good hap would have it chaunce;
> Thys devyll and I were of old acquaintaunce;
> For oft the play of Corpus Christi
> He hath played the devyll at Coventry.

Coventry's Devil was famous and acted as Porter at the gates of Hell and is also recalled by the drunken porter to the gates of Hell in *Macbeth*. In the mysteries, as in the quote, the devil pares his nails with a wooden dagger.

In *The Tempest*, Shakespeare refers to the dissolution, destruction of the great globe itself. The image of the massive paper globe being burned in Coventry's plays was remembered by everyone.

Hamlet's famous advice to players, telling them not to rant and ruin the play saying 'It out-Herods Herod, Pray you avoid it', can only allude to Coventry's Herod in his helmet, painted face and wig and falchion sword who ranted like a mad man. In directions from the Pageants themselves, a stage direction states, 'Here Herode ragis in the pagond and in the street also'. Coventry's Herod in the Shearman and Taylor's Play was remembered by all who saw him, including Shakespeare.

When Shakespeare has Judas greeting Christ with 'All Hail', this isn't from the bible but the Coventry plays. His reference to the cherubims dressed all in gilt is also from the mysteries.

The above shows that Shakespeare must have witnessed the Mystery Plays' probably on more than one occasion. A forgotten local tradition also says that Shakespeare visited Coventry for other reasons; it was claimed his interest here was in a young lady named Anne Whateley or Beck, who it is said he dumped when he found that his other Ann in Stratford was pregnant. It was suggested in the nineteenth century that the poet Bartholomew Griffin who lived in Coventry was known to Shakespeare as he was the first cousin of Alice Shakespeare of Wroxall.

Shakespeare came to Coventry for other reasons too, as an actor. It was a general practice in the Elizabethan/Jacobean period for travelling companies to perform Mayor's Plays. These were usually performed in guildhalls before the Mayor and Corporation who checked them for propaganda or insults to nobility and also to be privately entertained.

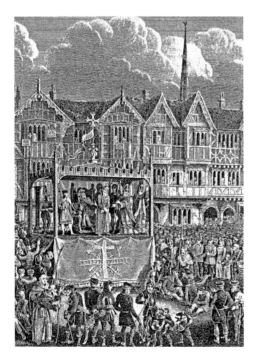

A fine early nineteenth-century engraving showing a pageant waggon playing Cross Cheaping around the time Shakespeare must have witnessed them.

If all was well, plays were given the go-ahead to be performed, probably in the hall or city. No particular inns in Coventry were noted as performance centres, except the Black Bull and the Angel, both in Smithford Street; at the latter we have a reference to the mayor complaining about its use for performance. But St Mary's Hall was, even in the days of the Mysteries, regularly used for rehearsals; the Smith's Accounts note in 1576, 'Paid for sent marye hall to reherse there ii d.'

I spoke to Joe Lancaster, a Shakespearean scholar a number of years ago, who agreed that the halls set up with side rooms mirrored the Shakespearean theatres in London. Indeed the halls use as a theatre continued into the eighteenth century when the great actress Sarah Siddons played there.

A description written by a certain Willis, born the same time as Shakespeare, talks of the procedure for actors playing in a city:

> In the city of Gloucester the manner is, as I think it is in other like Corporations, that when players of interludes came to town, they first attend the mayor to inform him what noblemen's servants they are, and so to get licence for their public playing. And if the mayor like the actors, or would show respect to their lord and master, he appoints them to play their first play before himself and the Aldermen and Common Council of the city; and that is called the Mayor's Play, where everyone that will, comes in without money, the Mayor giving the players a reward as he thinks fit to show respect unto them ...

This procedure certainly happened in Coventry, as Corporations accounts prove, and as at other guildhalls any play passed by the Mayor was likely to have been repeated in the hall, this time to paying customers. The fact that the Council's Chamberlains and Wardens Accounts show payments to the Lord Chamberlain's players, the Earl of Warwick's players and the Earl of Essex's players as early as 1575 suggests the guildhall was indeed used for the Mayor's Play and others. In July 1587 the council paid Lord Leicester's Players 20 shillings. September that year was a busy time for players in the city with the council making payments to the Earl of Sussex's Players and the Queen's Players, of which Shakespeare was thought to be a member, the sum of 31 shillings. In 1584 The Queen's Players with Shakespeare received a massive payment of 42 shillings. In 1590 they 'and the Turk' were paid 11 shillings, and in this year the 'Coventrie Players' were mentioned for the first time. In 1591 Shakespeare's group played the city in March and August and for their last performances got a massive 30 shillings.

There are suggestions that Shakespeare may have also served in the Lord Admiral Players in 1585, 1587 and 1590, who in those years received payments each time of 20 shillings from the council. Sources also suggest Shakespeare served in Lord Strange's Players in 1588 when the company played Coventry. It has also been suggested he was in the Earl of Pembroke's men in 1593 when they received a council payment of 20 shillings. Lastly, Shakespeare is believed to have served in the Earl of Worcester's Men when they played Coventry in 1576, 1578, 1579, 1582 and 1583. John Southworth, in his book, *Shakespeare the Player*, supports his inclusion in these groups. He points out that Worcester's Men visited Stratford on six occasions around the time Shakespeare left, giving him the opportunity to join the group. He also points out that his daughter Susanna

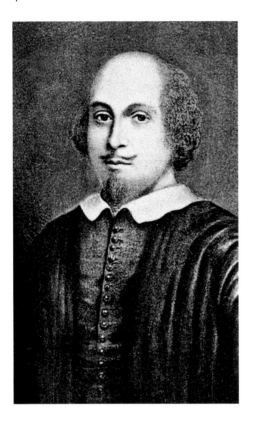

A fine image of Mr William Shakespeare, actor, playwright and poet.

would have been conceived when the group were in Stratford, and Worcester's Men were playing Coventry when Shakespeare got married. His twins were also conceived during the troupe's visit to Stratford and Coventry in 1583/84.

Coventry 1596 saw the Earl of Huntingdon's Bearward, Lord Willoughby's Players, the Queens Players, Sir Fulk Greville's Bearward, the Morris dancers of Stoneleigh, Lord Darcy's Players, Lord Ogle's Players, Earl of Derby's Players, Lord Admiral's Players and the Queen's trumpeters and the Earl of Essex's musicians all paid by the council. Musicians and singers were regularly in the city throughout this period. During the period of December 1599 to July 1600, nine groups of players played the city, that's a group performing in the city almost every month. After these council payments to the players it is recorded that Lord Chandos' Players were committed to prison 'for their contempt against maister maior'. It seems that Chandos' men's offence was playing at the Angel, 'contrary to maister maiors pleasure'. Had they bypassed the guildhall?

In 1603 fourteen groups of players were paid by the council, among them William Shakespeare made his return with the King's Men. This was said to be his last tour. In the year 1609 the city received ten visiting troupes in ten months. In 1616 seven companies performed for the council, also five groups of Waits (city musicians from Shrewsbury, Nottingham, Lincoln, Hertford and of course Coventry's own waits). On 21 December 1617 the council accounts actually name an individual; 'Paid unto Mr James Cranford for acting a comedy ... 33 shillings'. Interestingly, it isn't until 1635 that St Mary's Hall is

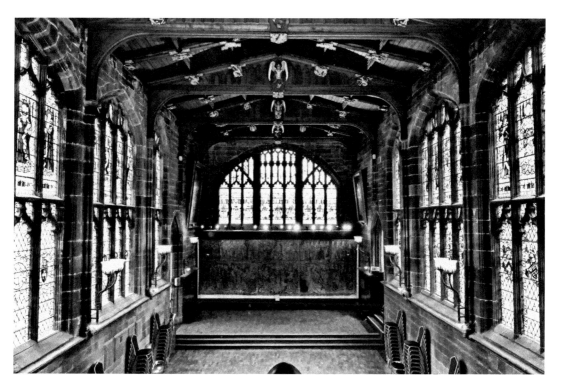

St Mary's Hall; a stage not only for Shakespeare but practically every noted company of the time.

named as the venue of the plays, under its other name, the Council House, as it was home to the council since the fourteenth century. The entry for 1636 from the Chamberlains and Wardens Account Book reads, 'Paid to the kings players of Blackfriars given at the Councel house in August last .... xx s'. In the same year the Queens Players are paid at the 'Parlor'; this is the Draper's Room in the hall, then known as the Mayor's (later Mayoress') Parlour. To be certain of the venue, we are told in 1637, 'Paid to the Players that came to the Councel House xx s.'

Not only did Shakespeare play Coventry and the Guildhall; numerous other groups did; all the best of the time visited the city making Coventry one of the top venues in the country for players. How many times they played we will never know. What we do know, however, is that Coventry with its Mystery Plays and regular visits from players and musicians was one of England's great centres of culture. One intriguing thought is as Shakespeare rehearsed and played in St Mary's he would knowingly be surrounded by many people who inhabited and were to inhabit his plays, Richard II, the Great Talbot, Henry V, Henry VI, and Richard III to name a few. Probably nowhere in any building he played could he see images of all these people around him. The question is did the hall actually influence his future plays?

5. Coventry and the Cult of Henry VI

Of all the monarchs who visited Coventry, none were as tightly linked to the city as King Henry VI and his Queen, Margaret of Anjou. During their period on the throne Coventry's history is linked into national history, through peace and war. Amazingly, Henry and Margaret between them visited at least thirty-nine times, spending over 2½ years based in the city, which became known as Margaret's 'secret harbour'. In 1459 the king and queen were in the city every month except for April. Henry struggled through his reign as others tried to take the crown and would ultimately be murdered; he would, however, rise again in the reign of Henry VII and Henry VIII as 'Saint Henry of Windsor', called by many, 'The Light of the World'.

Henry and his court actually lived in the city, making it literally England's capital. Throughout the Wars of the Roses the city, as best it could, kept its allegiance to the House of Lancaster. After Henry's death in the Tower, said to be at the hands of Richard of Gloucester (later Richard III) Henry's body lay in state at St Paul's where it bled 'anew' proving to the people that Henry had been murdered and had not died from 'melancholy and pure displeasure' as told by Yorkist propaganda. The body was quietly buried out of the way, at little known Chertsey Abbey, and within a short space of time miracles were being recorded.

Pilgrims started to flock to Chertsey to pray to 'Holy Henry', and soon statues and paintings of the king were created all over the country and venerated as holy images. In 1479 Edward IV issued a decree banning the veneration of images of Henry the 'Martyr'. The decree did not stop the growing cult and it continued into the reign of his alleged murderer, Richard III, who had the body removed to Windsor where he could control the growing cult. When the body was exhumed in 1474 it was said to be uncorrupted and smelling 'sweetly', proving once again that he was a saint. The miracles continued for those who prayed to the dead king.

Unlike his predecessors, Henry VII encouraged the veneration of his uncle, who he had claimed prophesised his coming and legitimised his claim to the throne. Henry, seeing the advantage of having an uncle who was a saint, approached the pope on the subject of his canonization. In 1494 a Commission of Enquiry was set up by Pope Alexander VI. This was continued by Pope Julius II in 1504, who informed Henry that the process could be speeded up by cash. Henry, however, not noted for giving away money, chose to wait.

The enquiry looked into the miracles attributed to Henry, a long list of which still survives among the Harleian Manuscripts. Most of these 300 recorded miracles belonged to the end of the fifteenth century; there were also 174 'wonders' attributed to Henry. Miracles attributed to Henry were many and varied and included a man who fell from a tower and prayed to Henry as he fell, he landed unhurt. Ships were saved from destruction and those nearly dead or even dead were brought to life by others offering prayers to the dead king.

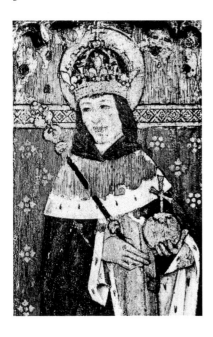

An image on a screen in Ludham church in Norfolk showing King Henry as a saint. This was one of many such images around the country.

Henry VII's chapel at Westminster Abbey was originally built to contain the shrine and body of Henry VI, but the translation of the corpse was blocked by the church at Windsor, who wanted to keep hold of his money spinning prestigious remains. The translation, however, did not take place, although Henry VII testified in his will that it was his intention to move the body.

Canonisation is a long process, especially when the cash isn't forthcoming, and Henry VII died not seeing its completion. The cult itself, however, continued to grow and hymns were written dedicated to Henry. Books of hours were produced, statues, panel paintings and stained glass. Pilgrim badges were produced in their thousands showing various images such as Henry holding orb and sceptre and standing on a lion or antelope. By 1499 Henry's cult had eclipsed that of Thomas Becket and a commission from the Vatican had, without difficulty, proved thirty-two miracles; you can become a saint with one. Henry's veneration was still going strong in 1529 for it is recorded that Henry VIII made an offering at his shrine in Windsor. Then Henry VIII wanted to remarry, England split from Rome and the canonisation and open veneration stopped. It was, however, restarted in the twentieth century.

The earliest surviving spread of the cult of Henry was found at York Minster where his former secretary, Dean Richard Andrew, erected a screen bearing images of English Kings from William the Conqueror to Henry VI. Henry's statue was being venerated by 1473.

Survivals of Henry's cult not surprisingly appear in Coventry and can still be seen in St Mary's Guildhall, considered to be the best guildhall in England. The great north window of the hall, the 'King's Window', was traditionally added in 1492. It is probably the work of the King's Glaziers at Westminster and chronologically contains images of Constantine the Great, King Arthur, William the Conqueror, Richard I, Henry III, Edward III, Henry IV, Henry V and Henry VI in the centre. This window, in all accounts of the hall, is simply described as bearing portraits of English kings, but as we can see it mirrors the images at the shrine of Henry at York. All of the kings depicted are Henry's ancestors, and Constantine and Arthur were his claimed ancestors.

The window was put in place in the reign of Henry VII and is dedicated to Henry VI, who through his auspicious ancestry legitimised Henry VII's claim to the throne. Also, four of the monarchs depicted were connected to the House of Anjou, and this is reflected in the fact that they bear the scalloped 'M' of Margaret of Anjou in the background. This is significant because Margaret could also claim connections through Henry's ancestors. Here we see Henry among conquerors, which may seem strange for a saintly man but the end of this prayer written down in 1508 says it all:

> O crowned king with sceptre in hand
> Most noble conqueror I may thee call
> For thou hast conquered I understand
> A heavenly kingdom most imperial.

There was also originally an image of Henry VI in the east window, but no description of the image survives.

Also, on the outside of the building underneath the windows are nine decorative niches, which once contained statues. What they were is not recorded, but I believe that like the statues at York, they mirrored the images in the window, with Henry VI in the centre. The destruction of these images is unrecorded, but if they were statues of monarchy, they certainly would have been pulled down during the Commonwealth.

Perhaps the greatest surviving relic to the veneration of Henry VI in England is also in the Guildhall hanging below the north window and is known as the *Coventry Tapestry*.

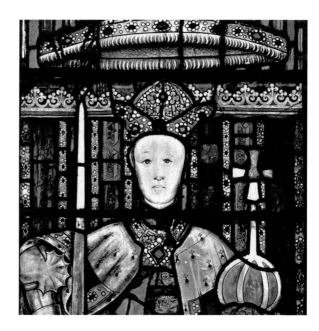

Henry VI in the King's Window in St Mary's Hall. The king appears very young in the window; a reflection on the fact that saints were often depicted younger than they really were. Apollonia in the tapestry below appears young and yet in reality she was old.

Before dealing with my interpretation of the tapestry we must look at its background. The earliest reference dates from 1519 when 26s 8d was spent on two men, 'it take upon them to me'de ye cloth of aras, by advice of M' Meir and his bred'. Also in 1604 a further forty shillings was spent on repairs. The first historian who could have mentioned the tapestry was Sir William Dugdale when he was in the Guildhall in 1653 researching his history of Warwickshire. Dugdale does not, however, mention the tapestry as it contained too much royal and religious imagery, which would not be allowed in Cromwellian England. The windows, however, despite depicting kings and nobility, were allowed to remain; perhaps the council decided it was too costly to replace the huge area of glass. And it was also said at the time that Kings and Saints were only any good for keeping out the draughts, so they were sometimes allowed to remain. As for the tapestry; it was cherished by the city fathers and put safely away.

The first known description of it is by historian and bibliophile, Humphrey Wanley, who mentions it in 1719. Stating, 'the upper end of the Hall is adorned by a very large and fine piece of Arras [tapestry], wherein are the Effigies of King Henry VI., his Uncle the Cardinal of England, and the Chiefest of his Nobility are represented. Above are many of the Apostles and the Saints as St George, etc. Against this King is his Queen Margaret, attended by her Ladies and protected by the Saints. Between them is the B.M.V. [Virgin Mary] attended by many Saints and Angels, and Justitia above her'. This identification was repeated by at least fifty historians into the twentieth century. Many believed the scene depicted showed Henry holding mass at St Michael's. Even George Eliot who uses the hall as the courtroom scene in Adam Bede refers to the tapestry depicting 'old kings and queens, unhappy, discrowned, imprisoned', she knew them to be Henry and Margaret, both were unhappy, uncrowned and both suffered imprisonment.

Because the tapestry was known to be Henry VI it was thought that the inhabitants of the tapestry wore clothes belonging to the reign of Henry VI, but later in the nineteenth century it was realised by Sir George Scharf that the tapestry, although depicting Henry VI, was actually made in the reign of Henry VII and the clothes belonged to that reign. A couple of less informed late nineteenth-century historians naively assumed that if the figures are wearing clothes of Henry VII's reign, then it must be Henry VII. At the turn of the century the then hall custodian, J. H. Welch claimed that a study of history gave its origin, then attacked its traditional identification and stated that the king and queen were Henry VII and Elizabeth of York. He said, 'no public body would be insane enough to place the tapestry in the hall some years after to commemorate such a wretched period in the history of England'. This gentleman obviously had not, as he claimed, studied his history for he knew nothing of the cult of Henry VI and its importance in Tudor England or the connection the Lancastrian court had to Coventry. Welch said there were Tudor roses on the tapestry and a mix of red and white roses in the border, saying this alone was 'fatal to the Henry VI theory'. Welch sowed the seeds of doubt on the figures in the tapestry based on uninformed opinion. The tapestry does not contain any Tudor roses, and as for red and white roses, the white roses are in reality faded red ones. The border does contain red roses for the house of Lancaster and red apples, symbolic of Anjou. They also appear in a tree before Margaret. Among the saints St Dorothea is also depicted, for she carries a basket of apples, which by miracle turned into red roses.

The majority of historians continued to identify the figures as Henry and Margaret through the twentieth century, then in 1948 the city archivist for eighteen months, Joan Lancaster, wrote a guide book saying that Sir George Scarf identified the figures as Henry and Margaret, then herself states, 'but in view of the probable date of its working, the tapestry is more likely to represent Henry VII and Elizabeth, while the costume supports the theory'. This conclusion again would suggest a lack of knowledge concerning the cult of Henry VI in the reign of Henry VII.

In 1983, thirty years after she left Coventry, she wrote a revised guide to the hall in which she links the tapestry into the 'well attested Tournai tapestries of *c*. 1500'. During conservation work in 2000 I spoke to a Tapestry Conservation Officer, from Hampton Court, who after close study of the tapestry was of the opinion that it was not crude enough for Tournai work and was Flemish. This was verified to me by tapestry expert Tom Campbell of the Metropolitan Museum, New York.

Lancaster, influenced by Welch, stated the 'Tudor roses in the border and the style of the costumes' confirms categorically that it is Henry VII. Once again the costumes cause confusion; in the upper lobby of the hall is a late seventeenth-century Antwerp tapestry in which men are depicted wearing Roman costume, this does not however mean that it was made in the Roman period. Using costume to date art can sometimes be a flawed science if the historical context of the subject is not understood.

In the 1983 guidebook there was more confusion about the Antwerp tapestry for Lancaster refers to it as being, 'difficult to place the Chinese figure'. This again is a misinterpretation, for the Chinese figure does not exist. It is in reality a metal shoulder plate with leather straps and sits on the shoulder of Pompey. The China man, like the Tudor roses in the *Coventry Tapestry*, does not exist, as with other things in the guide. There is, however, a single, now faded, red Lancastrian rose in a spandrel over the king's head, and behind him an apple.

Costume and roses, that was it; the argument for Henry VII was untenable. There is, however, much to be said for the original historical identification of Henry VI. There is a Flemish painting which shows remarkable similarities to the tapestry. Believed to date from the beginning of the sixteenth century it depicts the marriage of Henry VI to Margaret of Anjou. The artist has placed a halo around the dead king's head. Figures in the painting can be matched to those in the tapestry (some exactly). They are laid out in the same manner and may be based on a cartoon, an early evolution of the tapestry, made by an artist, attached to a Flemish workshop of weavers.

Now let's look at the tapestry itself. In each corner in a scroll are the initials 'H' & 'M' for Henry and Margaret verified by a professor of late medieval text. In the tapestry we have Henry kneeling in prayer, his favourite occupation, before him sits his crown and an open book. Importantly, the king looks upon the assumption of the Virgin Mary. Henry and the Virgin were the most important of the invocatory saints of the period. Henry looks upon the assumption and what was Christ in Glory as he did in life, for it was claimed that he had for three years running witnessed this vision; the cult of the Assumption was Henry's most favoured cult. The crown sits before the king bearing the five crosses, reflecting Henry's other favoured cults; the Holy Cross and the Five Wounds. The crown follows Henry's design but he does not wear it for he is in a state of grace and no longer king on earth. Above him stands St Paul, his sword hanging over his head, the sword of Damocles, symbol of Henry's doomed life on earth, also a symbol of the murdered monarch. Paul, however, looks and gestures towards heaven, for he will soon be a saint, or so everyone thought.

Next to the crown is an open book, the important right hand page is blank, symbolic of Henry's unfinished story. Opposite, above Margaret, stands the only royal saint, St Catherine. In her hand she holds a book, perhaps containing the names of the saints, she hold the symbol of her martyrdom, the sword, and with her index finger points directly down to Henry, linking herself to him, for soon he too will, like her, be a royal saint.

Around Henry's neck hang two massive gold chains, an anomaly in the king's life. Here we have pure symbolism; the massive chains are symbolic of imprisonment, Henry was twice imprisoned in the Tower of London, one loop for each confinement. On Henry's head is a red velvet cap, his favourite, later a sacred relic, Henry's red cap was believed to cure headaches and other mental disorders.

Kneeling behind Henry is Henry Beaufort, Bishop of Winchester, his uncle. Beaufort was the most powerful clergyman of the period, served two kings and sat at the trial of Joan of Arc. He was also richer than the king and paid much towards the upkeep of the royal court. He, like Henry VI, was a member of the Trinity Guild who owned the hall.

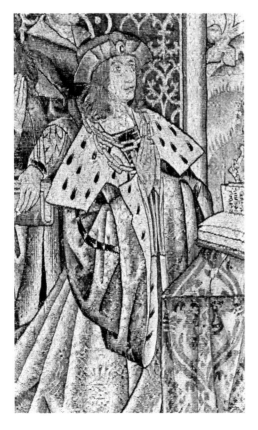

Henry VI as he appears in the unique Coventry Tapestry.

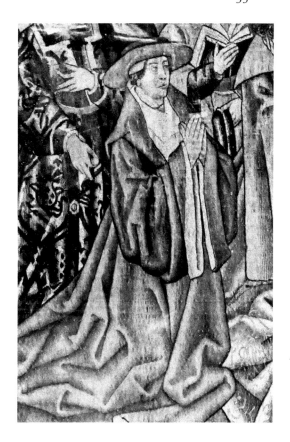

Right: Cardinal Henry Beaufort as seen on the tapestry.

Below: Beaufort's effigy on his tomb in Winchester.

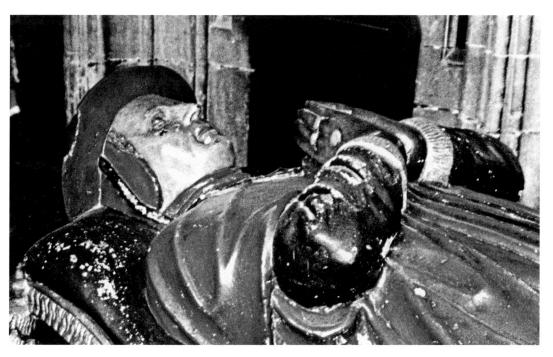

Standing behind the king holding a book is William de la Pole, Duke of Suffolk. His proximity reflects his importance, as Suffolk was the most powerful courtier in the land. He held numerous titles, as well as being the king and queen's favourite. He even married Margaret in proxy for the king in France and negotiated the marriage contract, which included handing over Maine and Anjou back to Margaret's landless father. This and his closeness to the king and queen would later prove his downfall, for when it became generally known his enemies came out and accused him of all sorts of misdeeds. Many, it was said, were jealous because Suffolk gained titles above others, including being the first non-royal to gain a dukedom.

Suffolk pleaded his innocence swearing that the return of Maine and Anjou was a council decision and not his personally. He swore his innocence twice before parliament and had a book compiled which refuted all the charges that were laid against him. The book now lost is now referred to as Suffolk's 'lost book'. I believe the figure in the tapestry shows Suffolk swearing his innocence to the Virgin, while in his hand he holds his famous 'lost' book.

Because of the attack on Suffolk Henry decided to banish his favourite for five years, no doubt thinking at an appropriate time he would call him back. Before leaving Suffolk again swore his innocence; he then wrote to his son refuting the charges against him. Suffolk had not long left the coast behind when he was stopped and taken aboard a ship called the Nicholas of the Tower. On board a mock trial was held and he was found guilty. The sailors then brought alongside a boat and Suffolk was beheaded on a block with a rusty sword. Above the figure of de la Pole in the tapestry is the figure of St Adrian standing on a lion symbol of fortitude, the badge of Suffolk. St Adrian is in armour (Suffolk was also a soldier) and is holding in his hands symbols of his martyrdom; a block

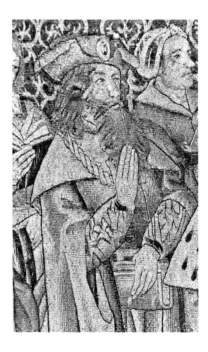

William de la Pole holding his lost book and swearing his innocence.

and, instead of an axe, his emblem, a sword. He is in fact displaying emblems of Suffolk's murder, considered by the Tudors as his martyrdom by Yorkist plots. Surprisingly Adrian, patron saint of soldiers and brewers, has pushed St Peter into the background, which goes against the rules of Christian art.

Behind Suffolk stands a figure whose interpretation is quite simplistic, for he holds an open book in his hand, which signifies that he is a writer or poet. In his right hand for no apparent reason he holds a cap; this is the clue, this is John Capgrave, court poet and author of the *The Book of the Illustrious Henries*. Capgrave has been described as the 'chronicler ... for whom Henry VI could do no wrong'. He was an Augustinian monk said to be the most learned of that order. Above Capgrave stands St George holding a banner which points at Capgrave. His connection lays in the fact that Capgrave was the first to promote St George in English. Capgrave even went on pilgrimage to the shrine of St George in Velabro. In the period the tapestry was made Henry VII tried to get Capgrave beatified.

Behind Capgrave stands another figure, which despite being in the middle of the group, stands aloof from them and looks away from the king. Above him is the only gap among the saints and a curious device, which looks like a piece of ancient script, reminding one of a snake. He stands in an unusual manner, leaning to one side, his left shoulder higher than the right. He holds his left hand in a crooked manner close to his chest and from his hand is a repair showing that he once probably held something, a snake, which reappears lower down kissing his finger ... the serpents kiss ... the kiss of the Judas, symbol of evil and cunning. In his right hand he holds a pile of coins, another symbol of the Judas. This is Richard III, Richard calls himself Judas at the end of Shakespeare's *Richard III*, and Bernard André, who wrote, 'Henrici Septimi Historia' said of him, 'The tyrant ... like a serpent that has fed upon noxious herbs.'

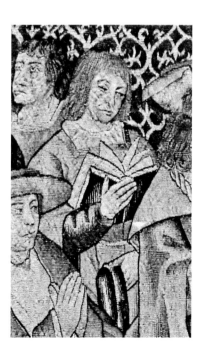

Court poet to Henry VI, John Capgrave.

Richard III, then Duke of Gloucester, was believed by the Tudors to have murdered Henry VI in the Tower. He was also one of the men who was believed by some of the Tudors to have killed the Prince of Wales. He stands as described by Holinshed, 'ill featured of limbs, crooked backed, his left shoulder much higher than his right'. He also has what some chroniclers describe as a crooked left hand. A Tudor portrait of Richard, known as the *Broken Sword Portrait* because the king holds a broken sword in his left hand, a symbol of his envisaged tyranny, mirrors the image in the tapestry.

This portrait belonging to the Society of Antiquarians is an almost exact copy of the image in the tapestry. It is said to be based on a portrait painted by Sir Thomas More, who called him a 'pestilent serpent', and was done while he was researching his history of Richard. Interestingly, More could have copied this image from the tapestry because he is known to have visited Coventry a number of times, for his sister lived here, she having married a Coventry man, the writer John Rastall, who published More's *The History of King Richard III* in 1557. During his research into Richard's life he may have visited the Guildhall to check documents kept in the Treasury. Maybe someone pointed out to him the image of Richard in the tapestry, the Judas, killer of kings and princes, standing there for all to see, so no one would forget. This may probably be the earliest image of Richard in existence and, interestingly, the hair colour is nearer to what DNA studies have proved than most of his later images.

On the far opposite side of the tapestry stands Anne Neville, daughter of the Earl of Warwick and companion of Margaret of Anjou, wife of Richard III. Before she was Richard's wife, she was the wife of Henry and Margaret's son Edward, Prince of Wales. Anne shows the whites of her eyes staring up at the figures above her. One is her own

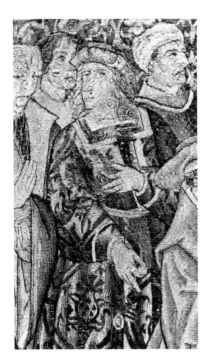

Richard III as he appears in the *Coventry Tapestry*. His identification is verified by John Ashdown Hill, who helped to discover the king's body. He also read the Latin prayer over the king's remains at his reburial.

patron saint, St Anne, and the one directly above her is St Apollonia, who was martyred by being thrown alive into a fire. She too looks up at a strange white creature with piggy ears and snout; a demonised version of Richard's emblem, the white hog. Here we have Anne Neville linked into Apollonia's death, forced into marriage with her husband's and father-in-law's murderer; and the man involved with her father's destruction at Barnet. It was suggested by some that Anne herself had been poisoned by Richard; in the Tudor mind cast into the fire with the devil himself.

Below her kneels her sister, Isabel, who was married to her husband's murderer the Duke of Clarence, and at their feet sit two dogs, Talbots. Anne and Isabel are nieces of the Great John Talbot, who we will meet shortly. Above Isabel stands her mother, another companion of Margaret of Anjou, and above her stands St Gertrude of Nivelle, above the Nevilles. Looking back on her sister Anne Beauchamp, wife of Richard Neville the Kingmaker, and her nieces, is Margaret Beauchamp, second wife of the Great Talbot and daughter of Richard de Beauchamp, 13th Earl of Warwick. Above her can be seen her aunt's daughter, Lady Eleanor Butler, daughter of Talbot and Margaret Beauchamp, standing between two nuns for she ended her days as a tertiary nun in the Carmelite order. Eleanor, it was claimed, and agreed by the act of parliament Titulus Regius of 1484, was 'stode maryed and plight trouth', to Edward IV; he did of course marry Elizabeth Woodville. This pre-contract was used by Richard III to illegitimise his nephews, the Princes in the Tower. Eleanor, the daughter of the Great Talbot, was seen at the time to have been ill used by Edward IV and his brother Richard III. All of these women were seen as victims of the Yorkists.

Mirroring Anne on the men's side of the tapestry we see a young man who is pulling back, holding his hand up to protect himself. He is being leered over by a dark haired man, the Duke of Clarence; an almost identical image with the same hairstyle appears on the Rous Rolls. This is the king and queen's only son, 18-year-old Edward of Westminster, Prince of Wales, the future of the Lancastrian cause. Some sources state he was killed on the field at Tewksbury, but other sources say he was captured after the battle and brought before Edward IV, who asked him how he dared to enter the realm with his banners flying, to which Edward replied that he had returned, 'to recover my father's crown and mine inheritance'. Then the chronicler states that Edward struck him with a gauntlet, and Richard of Gloucester, the Duke of Clarence and two other men killed him. Another version of this tale, more current when the tapestry was made, was that the Duke of Clarence with a small group of men discovered Edward grieving in a grove after the battle. Edward is said to have pleaded with Clarence, his brother-in-law, for his life but Clarence ignored his pleas and had him brutality beheaded. This latter story fits more closely to the tapestry as it shows Edward in fear of Clarence. Above Edward in the tapestry, standing holding a halberd, symbolic of battle (which points to Edward) is St Thaddeus or Jude patron saint of lost causes. Edward, the future of the Lancastrians, became a lost cause and like Thaddeus was beheaded.

Lastly among the identifiable are two male figures, before Edward. One is an old long bearded man and the second is a younger man pulling back his gown to show his purse. The elderly man gestures with his right hand to the younger man before him. His left hand, however, is resting, so it can be seen on the younger man's right shoulder. We now

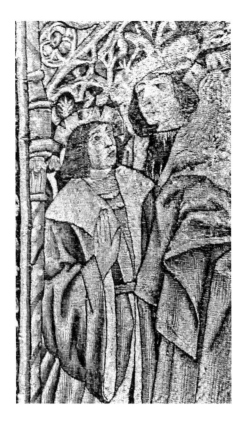

Prince Edward as he appears in the tapestry being threatened by Clarence.

know there is a family connection between the two men, and adding to this on the gown of the younger man is an upturned crescent. This is a cadency symbol, a heraldic device denoting number two and used to identify the second son. The device was formalised by Tudor heraldry around 1500. In this case this is the second son and second earl, hence the device.

What identifies the men is at their feet, a semi-passant dog; a medium-sized hunting dog called a Talbot, emblem of the Earls of Shrewsbury, the Talbots. The same dog can be seen behind the kneeling Earl of Shrewsbury in an illustration from the Shrewsbury Book showing the old earl presenting a book to Henry VI and Margaret of Anjou.

The older man is John Talbot, Earl of Shrewsbury, the greatest Lancastrian hero, referred to by Henry VI as, 'Talbott our good dogge'. Known as the 'Captain of England' the 'English Achilles', Shrewsbury won over forty battles. He visited Coventry a number of times and the people of Coventry gave money towards his ransom when he was captured at Patay. He died in battle in 1453, aged between sixty-nine and eighty at Castillion. Surrounded by a massive French army old Talbot told his son John, Lord Lisle to flee, but he refused and the two died together, leaving a heroic legacy behind. Between the two figures is another man mirroring their gestures; he may be John, Lord Lisle, for the saint over him is St Simon, whose main virtue is said to be loyalty, just as young John Talbot was loyal to his father ... to the end when their two bodies were found together, a well-known tale of the time.

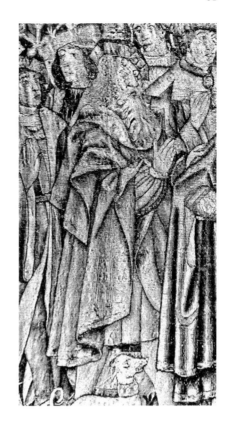

The Great Talbot, John Talbot 1st Earl of Shrewsbury, on the Coventry tapestry. Here he is seen as described in later life, blue eyed with long white hair and beard.

After Talbot's death the title then reverted, as shown on the tapestry by a cadency mark on his gown to the second son, yet another John. This John Talbot, who became Earl of Shrewsbury in 1454, pulls back his gown to show his purse, for in 1456 at the Coventry Parliament he was made Lord High Treasurer of England. He also paid off many of the king's debts and like his father and brother died in battle, at Northampton in 1460, with his brother Christopher. This almost mirrors that of his father and half brother. The heroic Talbots dying in Henry's cause were known to all.

Additionally, John Talbot gestures towards Richard, no doubt an allusion to the fact that his son, Sir Gilbert Talbot, aided the downfall of Richard by bringing 10,000 troops to bear against him at Bosworth and commanded Henry VII's right wing. In other words, the Talbots were a major factor in putting Henry VII on the throne. Interestingly, the son of this Gilbert owned Caludon Castle from 1485. Also the 2nd Earl's son, John the 3rd Earl, wrote a poem in praise of Margaret of Anjou and was a patron of the arts. He died in Coventry in 1473 aged twenty-five.

Finally, Queen Margaret of Anjou is depicted opposite and kneeling as the king. Before her lies open a completed book, her life was lived and she was now dead. Behind, through the tracery, is an open landscape in which stands a French castle, and before the castle an apple tree, symbolic of Anjou. The queen wears a dress similar to that in the Flemish Painting and on her head she wears a jewelled headdress. The headdress is decorated with black and tear drop pearls, symbols of mourning. Her husband and only son are murdered, and most significantly they give her name; the pearls are margaritas, this is Margarita de Anjou. The headdress is set back of her head in the French style. Significantly it consists purely of tall French *fleur-de-lys*, which, with the castle and apples, show this to be a French born queen. This has been added deliberately because all English queens are normally depicted wearing crowns of alternating crosses and small *fleur-de-lys*. Above the queen stands St Barbara, patron saint of soldiers and armourers, an interesting choice for a queen who for many years led armies in pursuit of her son and husband's birthright. Barbara's emblem is also appropriate; the tower, depicted in the tapestry as a white tower. Margaret spent her last five years in England as a prisoner in the White Tower in London before being ransomed for £10,000; she died in 1483, owning nothing but a few greyhounds.

Other things associated with Henry and Margaret in the Guildhall can be found in the ceiling, which features numerous chained antelopes, the badge of Henry VI, and chained swans, used as a badge for the Lancastrian party and by Margaret and Edward, Prince of Wales.

What we have at St Mary's Guildhall is what I believe to be the greatest surviving 'shrine' to Henry VI in England. The whole of the north wall and its window were adapted to take the Henry glass and the tapestry in the late fifteenth century when Henry's veneration was at a peak. The cult of Henry VI lasted for well over sixty years, outshining the great cult of Becket. The *Coventry Tapestry* is indeed rare, for it not only contains the two most revered figures of the period; it also doubles as a record of the struggles of the House of Lancaster. It is a special record which could only be made by a city so closely associated

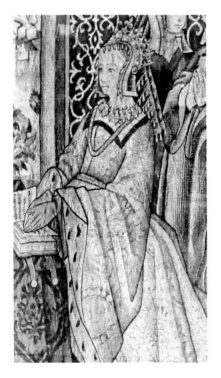

Margaret of Anjou as she appears in the tapestry of her 'Secret Arbour'.

to the royal family and court, for it is highly likely that everyone depicted did at some time live in the city and had been into the hall. There are still a number of unidentified individuals in the tapestry; the lady behind the queen is traditionally Lady Buckingham. Others must be, because of their close association with Coventry and the royals, Elizabeth, Lady Grey, Elizabeth, Duchess of Wiltshire and the widow of the 2nd Earl of Shrewsbury.

On the men's side we may have John Arundel, the king's physician and master of Bedlam, the Earl of Wiltshire and the Duke of Somerset, who like so many of the others sacrificed themselves for the royal cause; they could of course be construed as being martyrs to the cause. Who commissioned the great work? Some have tried to suggest Henry VII. He was however a 'notorious miser', who as king only spent about four days in the city and even had the city searched once for a gold spoon he had left behind, then when it was found gave no reward. He also promised to build a school in the city; he never did. The symbolism, however, on the tapestry I think says it all. Above Henry is St John the Baptist, over Margaret is St Catherine, and centre below is the Virgin Mary; they form a triangle, symbolic of the Holy Trinity, the name of these united guilds. I think this tells us who commissioned it; the Trinity guild and some of its most powerful members, who also formed the council. The tapestry is personal to Coventry; a record of Coventry's greatest moment when it became the home of a king and queen, a royal court and a saint, the guilds most famous member. It is also a statement of how the guild/council saw itself; men of power who could sit with saints and kings. The tapestry is older than any in Hampton Court, is unique and is in fact, with the King's Window, not only a Coventry treasure but a national treasure and yet remains little known. One could say amazingly, it's a secret.

6. Destroyed Buildings and Ones That Were Nearly Saved

One of the worst instances of an ancient building being rediscovered and destroyed is that of part of Cheylesmore Manor House. Many in the past referred to the timbered gateway as the manor house. This wasn't of course true ... half of Cheylesmore Manor House actually not only survived into the twentieth century, but also survived the war. Due to war demands, in 1942 a nearby engineering firm decided to expand its premises by knocking down an old building adjoining the gatehouse. Tiles were pulled off and ceilings ripped down revealing a complex ancient timbered roof with carvings. J. B. Shelton stepped in and halted the work and consulted buildings expert Philip Chatwin, who brought in an inspector of Ancient Monuments. Work was halted and the area where the tiles had been removed was covered. It was recommended by the Ministry that the building be listed as an Ancient Monument. Chatwin was pleased that the engineering firm were 'willing' to keep the ancient building preserved. In 1944 he wrote:

> The old half-timber building spanning the roadway has been always known as 'The Manor House.' No one seems to have realised that a row of cottages within on the left, crowned by ribbon weaving rooms, was actually the Hall of the Manor House, but such it has proved to be though its eighteenth-century disguise deceived us all. Admittedly there was the medieval chimney at the far end, but directly the plaster ceilings were removed the wonderful fourteenth century roof became apparent and further investigation showed that a few of the original timbers of the wall framing survived, built into the brickwork. The roof is undoubtedly a 'gem' and we look forward to the time when some of the old glory of the hall can be recovered. The roof is remarkable in two ways for not only is the timberwork a grand piece of medieval construction, but the tiles which covered it with its ridge complete are medieval too. Such a condition of things is unique in the Midlands and a very great rarity in the country as a whole. The tiles have been temporarily removed but, of course are being carefully preserved so no doubt when the reconditioning of this interesting old building takes place, as we hope it will after the war, they will be able to resume the useful work which they have done.

The most remarkable thing about the south and east ranges is that this medieval hall, which belonged to Queen Isabella and the Black Prince and visited by both, actually didn't survive and was demolished. The surviving wings of Cheylesmore Manor House, which actually dated back to at least 1250, was destroyed in 1956; it was said for 'necessary development'; so necessary the site stood untouched for over forty years and is only now partially occupied.

Local Historian Abe Jephcott, wrote to the press in 1955 pleading to save the building. His and many others' pleas were rewarded when the building was scheduled for

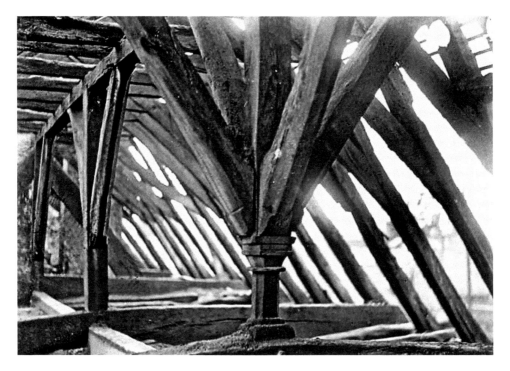

The fine-timbered roof of Cheylesmore Manor House. All that survives is this photograph!

preservation but despite this, Cheylesmore Manor House was demolished in 1956. Why? Because this time it was said to be unsafe. The gatehouse fortunately survived and was restored in the 1960s.

Coventry Castle has intrigued people for centuries, and for centuries many antiquarians wrongly linked it with Cheylesmore Manor House site. This mistake was carried through into the twentieth century despite the clues. There are still some who, despite the evidence, refuse to believe Coventry had a castle, using logic like; if there was a castle why are there no remains? My answer to that is, you can find around the country many castle sites where nothing remains; look at Liverpool. Coventry is not however such a site.

Coventry Castle dates from the time of the Barons' Wars between Stephen and Matilda. There is a reference in the *Anglo-Saxon Chronicle*, under the date 1137, which states, 'For every great man built him castles and held them against the king; and they filled the whole land with these castles. They sorely burdened the unhappy people of the country with forced labour on the castles, they filled them with devils and wicked men'.

Ranulf Gernon, Earl of Chester was such a man for the chronicle continues under 1140;

Thereafter very great strife arose between the king and Ranulf, Earl of Chester ... The earl held Lincoln against the king and deprived him of all he ought to have. The king went thither to besiege him ... and the earl stole out and went to get the assistance of Robert of Gloucester.

Robert and Ranulf returned with a large force and Stephen was captured and taken to Bristol where he was imprisoned. In 1142 the king and Ranulf were reconciled and swore oaths not to deceive one another. This lasted until 1146 when Stephen had Ranulf imprisoned.

It was during the period 1137 to 1140 that the earl no doubt enslaved the local population into building him a motte and bailey castle, consisting of a wooden keep on a mound encircled by a wooden stockade and ditch. The motte would have stood at the highest point overlooking Broadgate, encircled by what is now High Street, Pepper Lane and Hay Lane, below Bayley Lane and Earl Street; these mark the bailey of the castle.

The first attack on Coventry castle was led by Earl Robert Marmion of Tamworth, a man, 'great at warre'. A supporter of Stephen, he arrived in Coventry in late August 1143, drove the monks from the Priory and began to dig ditches and mantraps in the area between the Priory and the castle. It is interesting that in 1938 while underpinning the walls of Blue Coat School a number of skeletons were found huddled against an old wall where they had laid for centuries. Their position suggested that they had been buried together. Cleavages in the skulls of several of them appeared to have been caused during lifetime and not since the burial of the bones. Who were these men put to the sword? Victims of ensuing battles to take the castle, or perhaps our man of war didn't simply drive the monks out but got rid of them the only way some men of war know how.

Marmion fortified the priory, watched from the castle by Earl Ranulf's men. He dug in, waited and then took to riding out alone daily, defiantly parading himself before the castle. This continued until one day, soldiers suddenly spilled out of the castle. Caught unaware, Marmion made a dash back to the priory, and in the panic his horse came crashing down into one of his own mantraps. There are two versions of what followed; one says that he was decapitated by a common foot soldier, the second version says he lay in the ditch for some hours his leg broken and was dispatched by a cobbler. Considering though that at this point he was being pursued by soldiers the first account is most likely.

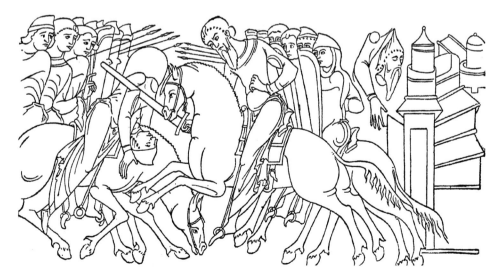

Soldiers at the time of the Barons' War.

What is most interesting about this event is that Marmion, a supporter of Stephen, attacked Ranulf's castle, after Ranulf and Stephen had been reconciled; this reconciliation didn't break down until 1146. So why was Marmion attacking the earls castle? There is a surviving earlier charter, which claims that Ranulf had handed Coventry over to Marmion. If Marmion believed he held the right to Coventry he probably came to claim it and Ranulf, as he sometimes did, changed his mind. This was probably why Marmion attacked. Later Marmion's sons claimed real rights to Coventry given to their father by Ranulf.

In 1146 Stephen imprisoned Ranulf and later released him, on condition, as the *Anglo-Saxon Chronicle* states, 'that he gave hostages and swore on holy relics to yield up all his castles. Some he did yield up, but others he did not'. One of the castles he yielded was Coventry. Ranulf proved again, however, that he could make and break oaths. He quickly gathered a force and began to retake his castles and others belonging to the king. *The Deeds of Stephen* (Gesta Stephani) written shortly afterwards tells us that Ranulf 'passed rapidly from one region to another with his unbridled army and by his ravages turned everything into desert and bare fields'.

King Stephen now owned and occupied Coventry Castle and Ranulf came to retake it. Gesta Stephani tells us that,

> Also in front of the Castle of Coventry, whither the kings men had withdrawn, the earl himself fortified a castle and valorously checked their sorties over the country, until the king arrived escorted by a fine and numerous body of knights, gave the garrison fresh supplies, of which they were in the greatest need, and fought a number of engagements with the earl, who had laid ambushes for him at the most difficult points of his journey.

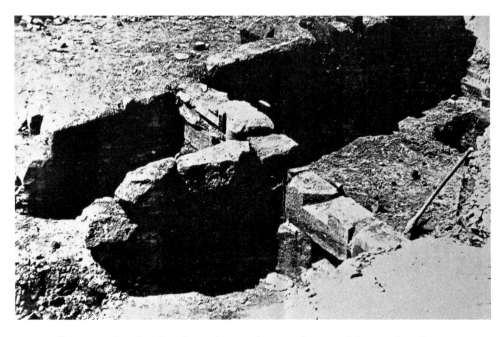

Large wall uncovered on the edge of Broadgate with arrow slit. Part of the actual castle entrance?

The Deeds inform us that the first conflict resulted in heavy casualties, and prisoners were taken. The king himself was wounded and yielded ground to Ranulf. Later Stephen rejoined the fight and Ranulf himself was nearly killed and eventually put to flight. The Deeds continue, 'he at length obtained the surrender of the earl's castle and demolished it'. This last reference to the earl's castle being demolished has been taken by all historians as referring to the destruction of Coventry Castle. This is wrong, and what Stephen actually demolished was the earl's siege castle. Coventry Castle, that is King Stephen's castle, was left untouched.

Reconciliation must have been agreed, for in Stubb's Charter mention is made of an agreement made around 1147–1151 between Ranulf and Robert of Leicester, in which they agree that no more castles would be built between Coventry and Leicester. This was to make sure that Stephen ultimately controlled the area and wasn't threatened by any new military incursions there. After Ranulf's death Coventry Castle must have initially still lay in royal hands but was reacquired by the lordship of Chester by Ranulf's son Hugh. In Hugh Keviloc's 'boundary charter', he refers to 'lata(m) porta(m) mei castelli'; the broad gate of my castle.

As mentioned earlier, when Keviloc rebelled against Henry II in 1173, Coventry Castle was placed under siege by Richard de Lucy. This siege, which resulted in a victory for the king, meant that the castle suffered considerable damage; this was probably the beginning of the end of the castle. The last mention we have of the castle is in a charter of around 1199–1204 when Ranulf Blundeville forbids his constables to bring burghers into the castle to plea their causes. The constable was of course responsible for the castle in the absence of the lord, which could be for considerable periods of time. A cartulary deed of 1144–1146 informs us that Eustace Fitz John granted property near the south gate in Coventry. This grant appears just after Eustace became Constable of Chester and is particularly interesting because of the south gate; the city had no gates or walls at this time, so it could only be the south gate of the castle. It was normal for castle constables to occupy a building near or in the castle entrance.

There is another reference in the Eyre Rolls in 1262 to the late Herman Attcastelgate. It was normal in this period for people to sometimes take their surname from a landmark where they lived; this suggests that Herman lived in a house by the castle gate, probably in Broadgate. So we now have suggestions for two gates into the castle. Part of the area around the lower end of Bayley Lane was referred to in the Coventry Leet Book as the 'Stiltyard', this is an obvious corruption of tiltyard, an area in a castle in which they could tilt (joust). Above this area when the municipal building was under construction in St Mary's Street in the 1850s, it was written, 'Half a dozen feet below the surface, behind St Mary's Street, some stonework has been found ... indicating the existence there of a very early building.'

As previously mentioned the first castle would have been a motte and bailey, with the motte (mound) between Hay Lane (Haeg meaning enclosure) and Broadgate. The bailey ran down the hill and the course of the ditch appears to be mirrored by the present Bayley Lane. The hill originally would have been much higher than it now appears, for St Mary's Hall stands on its original fourteenth-century level and lower down in Bayley Lane excavations showed the same level to be about twelve feet deeper, showing a considerable drop in the original hillside.

There is however a second ditch, which suggests a square keep belonging to a later stage of the castle, this time made of stone. This ditch was referred to in a charter of 1293–97 as 'fossatum castelli', the castle ditch. It was unearthed in 1894 and described as being 25 feet deep and full of black mud. It runs from Earl Street, across the High Street and under shops in Hay Lane, curving sharply and cutting under the north-west corner of the tower of St Michael's. It was noted in the past that the tower began to lean slightly, and when work took place in the nineteenth century to underpin it workmen found that it stood on a ditch cut into the bedrock. The ditch was deep, and in it were remnants of a building and gravestones, believed to be Norman. These were probably the remains of the original Norman chapel which stood in the bailey of the castle. Similar remains, including a gravestone, were dug up under the east wall of St Mary's Hall in the 1870s. The ditch runs through the centre of St Michael's and comes out under the central buttress of the east end. This buttress appears to have been added because of poor foundations, and in the middle of the nineteenth century a hole was dug here and the castle ditch found. Workmen dug through 26 feet of rubble before they gave up trying to find the bottom. This proves that the original chapel did indeed sit within the castle bailey.

The Langley Cartulary refers to it as, 'in ballivo qui ducit ad ecclesiam sancti Michaelis', the church of St Michael's in the bailey. Another reference to the bailey is a charter (c. 1220s) of William Crude, who gives to God, St Mary and the monks of Comb, 12d forever from rent to land in Coventry in the Bailey (in Balliva). This was a few years after the destruction of the castle. It appears that by this time the earl had sold off the land of Coventry Castle, except an area in 1307 called the Earls Garden. In Castle Yard, Bayley Lane was excavated recently the castle bake house with its ovens. The 'castelbachous' was mentioned in *The Pittancer's Rental*, 1410/11, and twice in the Corporation Deeds. They generally were outside the main wall for fear of fire.

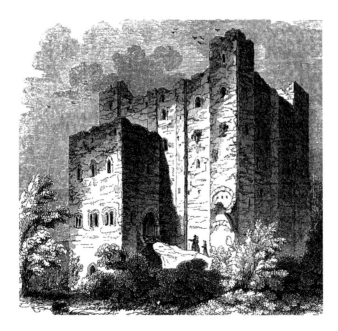

A typical Norman castle with tall square keep. Others had shorter keeps. Coventry's second phase was in stone.

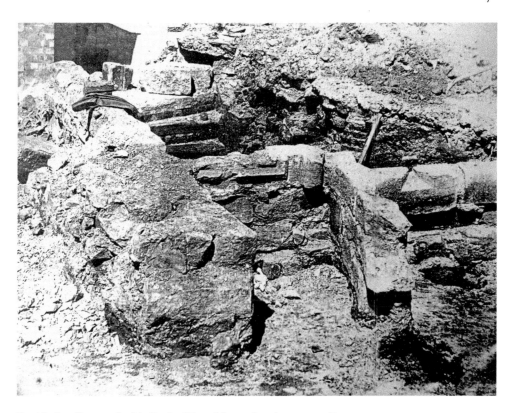

Fortified wall unearthed in Derby (Tyrrel) Lane showing arrow slit.

This second stage of the castle was of the later Norman type with square keep and single hall (with no motte) and outbuildings. The defensive ditches of this castle were mainly squared requiring the first ditch to be mainly filled and recut. Entrance to the castle was gained over the ditched gate at the top of Broadgate, near Pepper Lane, part was excavated in 1974 and measured 24 feet wide and 21½ deep. The ditch was dated to the mid-twelfth century by two shards of Stamford Ware. Then it continued through a secondary defence in now gone Derby Lane, which was once called Tyrrel Lane, a name linked to defensive works; and indeed a massive wall was unearthed here with arrow slits. Then across a second ditch, which lies under Hay Lane and completely encompasses the keep, then through a double entrance gate.

There appears to have been much defensive stonework out towards Broadgate. It was reported in December 1918, when the Craven Arms was under reconstruction in the High Street, that excavations revealed a solid stone wall about six feet thick. Nearby excavations also revealed remains of a moat. This massive stone wall passed under the buildings adjacent to the Craven Arms on the east side and was then lost. Historian William Fretton said that the wall could be seen in the undercroft near the entrance to the Rose and Crown yard, now the Courtyard and on the corner of High Street and Little Park Street also traces of a moat were found. The wall at this point disappeared and was thought to turn in a southerly direction towards where Coventry Castle was located. Other stone structures have been unearthed towards Broadgate including the base of a tower. This stone castle may have been more complex than we realised.

In the past some have suggested that St Mary's Guildhall contains remnants of the castle. It is firstly noticeable that the hall appears to be constructed mainly from robbed stone, both ashler grey and old red sandstone all thrown together in no order. John Stowe mentions in the late sixteenth century, 'a fortelet or pile [still] standing in the Earles streete, where the Earles of Chester did make their abode, whiche they afterwards decayed and turned into tenements', here is the source of the mixed stone. Originally, parts of the building would have been made from one stone only, old red sandstone from Coventry, with later additions from ashler grey from the south. When the building was being demolished these stones would be used as they came, as we see in the guildhall. In the great hall near the roof and in the gatehouse can be seen very large stones which are totally out of context with normal building procedure; big at the bottom, small at the top. This suggests that these larger stones, put in around 1396, were stones from the base of another building nearby ... Coventry Castle.

Caesar's Tower is very interesting, for this has been linked with Coventry Castle and the rebuilt tower previously showed signs of considerable age, older than the main hall. The tower was first mentioned in a deed of 1393 defining the boundaries of the site, saying that St Mary's Hall extends, 'to the corner of the South Tower'. The question is, which corner, as this suggests that the tower, as many have thought, was separate.

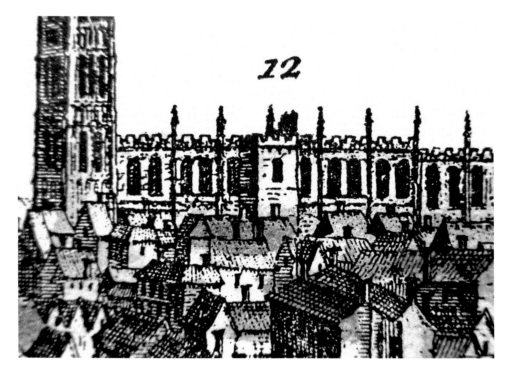

A 1731 engraving showing a Caesar's Tower (below fig. 12) when it was four storied and was topped by battlements and a turret.

Caesar's Tower is a name normally found attributed to castle towers. In 1900 the base of the now largely rebuilt tower was excavated and dated to the mid-twelfth century. This dating was based on the plinth of the tower, compared with other Norman towers, and the fact that the stones bore the marks of an adze; a tool normally used by Norman masons. It was also noted in the 1930s that the tower had other Norman characteristics.

It was not totally unknown for medieval buildings to have square stone towers. Caesar's Tower is, however, different. Apart from the fact that it was always said to predate the building that it's now attached to, it is wedge-shaped, not square, and unlike the hall it was made of only one type of stone. It was also originally four storied with battlements and an embattled turret; these battlements were already ruinous in 1471 when they were repaired. So we originally had a tower up to seventy feet high with battlements and bow apertures and a look out turret; a feature only found on castles. This was facing towards the ditch and exactly in line with the top of Broadgate, the site of the portam. If we mirror this wedge-shaped tower we create a funnel entrance, a killing zone. Early images of the original tower show that it had a line of massive postholes about half way up. This could suggest a wooden structure, joining two free standing towers, above the entrance and supplying murder holes and a defensive point. Many forget just how much heavy woodwork was employed in defences in early castles.

The tower has the lower part of a wall, possibly part of the original curtain wall, running underneath the Prince's Chamber; everything above is later infill. This wall appears to have lost half of its original thickness. Assuming this was the line of the curtain, which by the way mirrors the line of the ditch in Hay Lane, its position would show some relevance to the door arrangement in the tower. The tower doors are exactly where one would

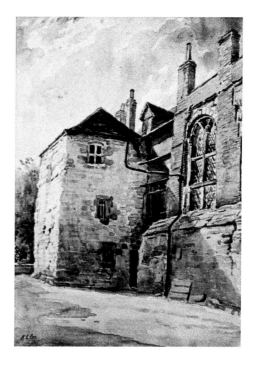

A Cox watercolour showing Caesar's Tower before restoration. Interestingly, almost the entire tower is built of ashler grey, not a stone found in Coventry quarries.

expect them to be on a castle tower. The first at the base of the curtain, the second, left of it, originally approached by an exterior stair, and the third in line with the curtain wall. This third door is very important, for it is very low and was recorded as being so in the fourteenth century. This is a defensive doorway made low, so if the battlements are breeched anyone entering this room would have to bend down putting them at a disadvantage and making them vulnerable. The fourth story would be entered from the third floor through an opening in the ceiling. There is a remnant of a newel staircase, but this may be a later addition.

Up until the late nineteenth century remains of a wall was part of a second kitchen beyond Caesar's Tower. This was of unknown date, and being at least 6 feet thick suggests a connection to the castle. During renovation work in 1914 on the south-east corner of the kitchen a large crack caused workmen to expose the foundation with the intention to underpin it. Below was, 'revealed an enormous mass of masonry'. Workmen tried to find the bottom of this masonry and gave up at 12 feet. Lastly, in the undercroft of the hall are two wells. These could of course have originally supplied the castle. More stonework is mentioned by T. W. Whitley, who stated in 1884 that somewhere around Bayley Lane was unearthed 'a large stone wall of great strength ... with much fallen stone around it'. During the clearing of the ground at the rear of the hall for the council house literally tons of stonework was carried away and with it much archaeology. It was said at the time that a book could be written on all that was unearthed here. Sadly nothing was written. It was noted at the time that bones had been found well below an undisturbed strata containing twelfth-century pottery.

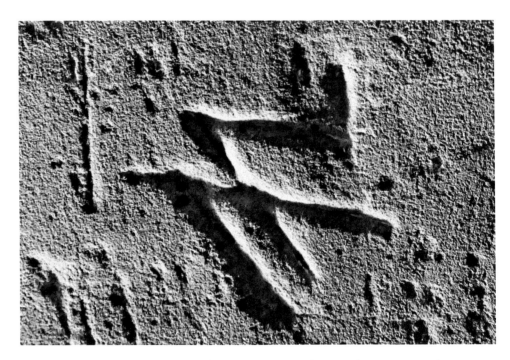

The surviving small section of the wall in Caesar's Tower bears eight ancient ritual protection marks, the VV. Was this to protect the Treasury or the Castle?

It is thought Coventry Castle fell from use around 1215, when King John ordered the slighting of castles which could be held against him. As he already held Kenilworth, Coventry Castle would be expendable. I believe that Coventry Castle at this point was probably already in ruins. As I mentioned earlier, the last siege in 1173 may have caused major damage. Add to this Ranulf Blundeville's charter dated around 1199 to 1204, which prohibits burghers being brought into the castle. Here we could be seeing the end of the castle; after war damage the earl may have decided to wind down his interest in Coventry Castle, beginning with non entry, then demolition and sale of land. Despite the sale of castle land, a small area called the 'earl's garden' is referred to in 1307. This does not of course mean that it still belonged to the earl, for Ranulf died in 1232; it is a memory of the bailey or possibly a castle meadow.

Coventry Castle's short and bloody history left its mark on Coventry, even to the present day, with Broadgate, the latam portam, of the Earl of Chester's castle.

A much loved Coventry building was the fifteenth-century Palace Yard, which once stood in Earl Street. Its most noted owners were the Hopkins family. Possibly the first Hopkins in the Yard was Richard, who was sheriff of Coventry in 1555. Richard, a draper, was a devout Protestant and was put out of office in the reign of Bloody Mary for having sympathies for Robert Glover, who was later martyred. Hopkins had refused to torture him and wanted him set free. For this he was placed under scrutiny and later arrested for giving an unauthorised religious book to a condemned felon in prison. He was seized and thrown in the Fleet Prison.

The martyr John Bradford wrote:

When was it read that sheriff of a city hath suffered for the Lords sake? To the end of the world it shall be written for a memorial to your praise that Richard Hopkins, sheriff of Coventry, for conscience to do his office before God, was cast into the Fleet, and there kept prisoner for a long time ...

Hopkins was not, however, destined to martyrdom as he had powerful friends, and through them he was set free. With his wife and his eight children he passed the remainder of Mary's reign in exile at Basle, Germany before returning to Coventry.

Richard was followed by his son Nicholas. He too was a draper, and his house was often referred to as 'Mr Hopkins' house by the Drapery door. The son of Nicholas was Sampson, he was a puritan and Mayor of Coventry in 1610, also Member of Parliament in 1614 and 1621. He left money for three sermons to be preached annually in St Michael's, one fell on the anniversary of the Gunpowder Plot. This was, of course, because it was during his residency that the Princess Elizabeth was kept under armed guard in the house to protect her from the Catholic Gunpowder Plotters. His residency in the 'Yard' is confirmed in Smythe's Lives of the Berkeleys that in May, 1596, the body of Lady Katherine Berkeley, before it was conveyed with great ceremony to St Michael's for burial, rested at the house of Sampson Hopkins in Earl Street.

Sampson's eldest son, William, later Sir William, was an ardent Royalist in a family that lived in Parliamentarian Coventry. He is said to have been a Grammar School master on the Isle of Wight, and in 1648 became involved in plot to break King Charles I out of

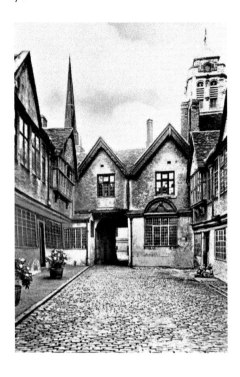

The first courtyard of Palace Yard looking towards the council house. The entrance to the yard was opposite to the last bay of the council house.

his imprisonment in Carisbrooke Castle. The scheme went awry when the authorities got wind of the plot to effect the King's escape by the aid of a 'little ancient man and a lusty stout young man about twenty-six or twenty-seven years of age', William Hopkins and his son being probably the conspirators to which allusion is made.

Sampson's third son was Sir Richard Hopkins (1612–1682) of Palace Yard, whose initials RHS with his wife and arms appeared on much of the house's decorative lead work. Sir Richard corresponded with both Charles I and Charles II before the Restoration. He was Steward of Coventry and was later chosen to present to the king a silver basin and ewer, worth 150 guineas, and purse of gold. Sir Richard died in 1682. His younger brother, Richard, lived till 1707, and lies buried in St Michael's with his son Edward, last of the Hopkins to represent Coventry.

Richard acquired the house because his elder brother had mortgaged it off to support the Royalist cause. It was most likely Sir Richard (the third son of Sampson), who beautified the south, or Palace, end of the courtyard with a fine ceiling in the old State-Room. It was divided by cross beams into four panels and each panel was filled with a laurel garland. Tradition says this was the room where James II held his Court on 1 September 1687 when he, wishing to reconciliate the Whigs, chose to stay not at Whitefriar's with the Hales', who were Tories, but at Whig, Richard Hopkins', house. This Richard, the eldest son of Sir Richard, sat in parliament six times. He actually accompanied the king personally from Daventry. King James made no friends by his efforts and offended the Corporation in the manner he received his Coventry Cup, a cup of massy gold worth £200 which they presented to him. This he passed on to Colonel Legge whose father had been imprisoned in the city during the Civil War. Edward,

Richard's son, later wrote of the event, 'King James lay at my father's house, where the morning after his arrival, public mass was said in the great dining room, where I was present at the late celebration of it ...'

The next morning James touched 300 people for the King's Evil (scrofula) in St Michael's Church, and after a 'stately breakfast' in St Mary's Hall departed. Next year he was a fugitive, and his daughter, Princess Anne, also a guest of Richard Hopkins, joined his enemies. Princess Anne visited Palace Yard in 1688 for two days. This Richard died in 1707 and was buried in St Michael's. He was succeeded by his eldest son Edward, who was MP for Coventry and Secretary of State for Ireland. He also lies in St Michael's. His son Richard continued as MP for Coventry and was Lord Commissioner for the Admiralty and of the Treasury. Edward died without issue in 1799. The family left Palace Yard in 1781, and in 1822 a relative, Lt-Gen. C. Northey Hopkins, sold it.

In 1851 an Auctioneer's sale bill advertised the Yard for sale. It is described thus; 'Lot 1. – All that capital and Roomy INN called or known by the Sign of The Old Golden Horse Tavern, situate in Earl Street, with the Stables, Brewhouse, and other Premises, now occupied by Mr John Lloyd, together with two Pieces of Land fronting to Earl Street, suitable for the erection of two retail shops and ample Yard room behind, having a long frontage and a proposed thoroughfare Road, to be called the Old Palace Court'. It was noted at the time that a painted board could still be seen under the arch giving arrival and leaving times for stage coaches.

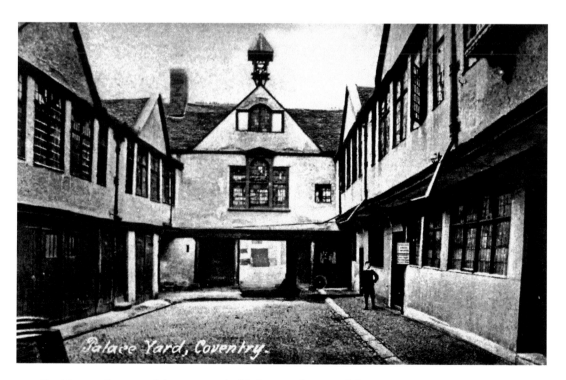

Palace Yard, Coventry.

Looking to the rear of the courtyard of Palace Yard. Beyond this were originally outbuildings, gardens and other courts.

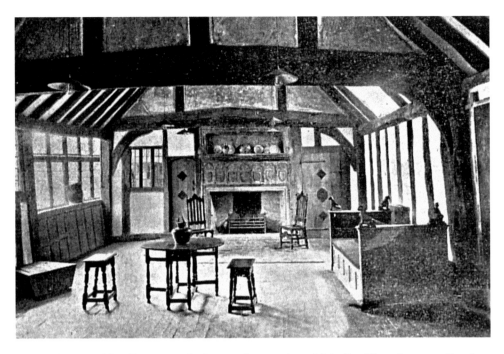

The newly restored first floor room of Palace Yard's west wing with its fine fifteenth-century fireplace.

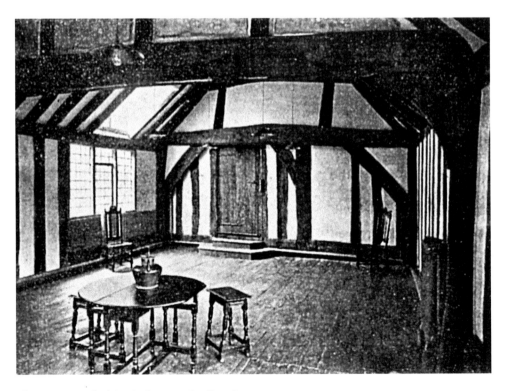

The same room looking in the opposite direction.

The title of Palace Yard wasn't the original name of the Hopkins' house in Earl Street. The building, since its sale, had served as Miss Sheldrake's school for young ladies, an inn, and builder's premises, and part of it was let as a residence and other portions as offices. The actual house itself became the Golden Horse with its courtyard known as the Golden Horse Yard. It was actually Mr Ackroyd, a builder, who created the name, more as a business address than from its historic associations. He advertised the place as 'Palace Yard' in about 1850. He thought Elizabeth I had stayed there.

In 1915 the building was under threat of demolition and a plea for its preservation was made by historian Mary Dormer Harris in an article in 'Country Life'. She wrote, 'there exists no town house of this type and importance in England – save, maybe, the New Inn at Gloucester – better worth preservation; and yet the fear is always imminent that the site may fall to a property speculator, and the glories and memories of Palace Yard vanish'.

It was saved by George Singer of Singer Cycles. He died and it was offered by his executors privately and cheaply to the council as it was thought that they would wish to save this important building. They, however, turned the offer down. In 1918 the property came under threat again and letters appeared in the press from all over the country pleading that it be saved, many again pressed the council to save it. William Coker Iliffe said he would purchase the property for £8,000, 'in favour of the Corporation for the same sum plus legal charges'. The Corporation thanked him and again turned down the offer. Besides, it was pointed out it could take three to four thousand pounds to restore it.

In April 1918 Palace Yard had been purchased by a trust, a group of Coventry citizens, including Iliffe. This was led by Bishop Yeatman-Biggs for the Bishopric of Coventry; its future was secured and restoration got underway. Yeatman-Biggs died in 1929 and a plaque was unveiled in the James II room in his honour. Despite its assured future, on 14 November 1940 bombs removed this beautiful building from the face of the earth; its destruction complete in mere seconds, it now lives only in memory.

The home of Orlando Bridgeman was once one of the finest in the city. In the late nineteenth century antiquarian William Fretton wrote that he believed it stood in the middle of Little Park Street next to the Banner House. 'Its demolition', he said, 'was inexcusable; it was not in the way, and the reason for its removal I have never been able to learn. It was a handsome, half-timbered mansion, with two gables in the street, and two to the court on the south side, with two large bays the street front of two stories'. This fine building was originally built by Sir Simon Norton, a dyer, in 1610, and was afterwards occupied by Lord Berkeley and Sir Orlando Bridgeman. Then it became the property of silk manufacturer Mr William Bird, whose descendants had it taken down and sold around 1820.

Fretton's belief that it stood next to the Banner House was backed by other historians; they even believed that originally Banner House may have been part of it. There was also a bowling green behind the Banner House known as 'Lady Bridgeman's Bowling Green'. Moreover, beneath the quite modern property which then adjoined Banner House were ancient stone cellars, which would fit a large mansion.

Bridgeman's grandfather was bishop of Chester, his father was Lord Keeper of the Great Seal under Charles I. At the Restoration he became Lord Chief Baron and presided over the trials of the regicides. Orlando Bridgeman was returned at the Horsham

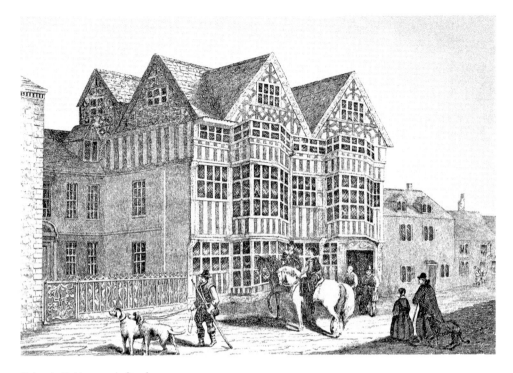

Orlando Bridgeman's fine house.

by-election in 1669 and created a baronet. The warrant for his baronetcy gave his address as Cheshire, although it was noted at the time that he preferred to live in his house in Little Park Street, Coventry. Orlando Bridgeman died in 1701 and was buried at St Michael's church.

His son, another Orlando, succeeded his father's baronetcy and estates in 1701, and in 1705 he ran as a Whig candidate in Coventry but was defeated. Probably during these periods he used his father's old Coventry house as a base. He won his second election in 1707 and was re-elected in 1708. The election was contested and in March 1709 he was confronted with accusations of bribery and corruption but cleared. He was defeated in Coventry in 1710 and never stood in the city again. His continuing expenses on his country house at Bowood caused him much difficulty. In 1738 he was made Governor of Barbados and soon after he feigned his own suicide by drowning. The Lord Egmont wrote:

> Sir Orlando Bridgeman who, instead of going to his government of Barbados conferred on him last winter, made his escape (as he hoped) from the world, to avoid his creditors, by pretending to make himself away, and accordingly gave it out that he had drowned himself, was ferreted out of his hole by the reward advertised for whoever should discover him, and seized in an inn at Slough, where he had ever since concealed himself.

He was buried on 5 December 1746, having died in Gloucester Gaol.

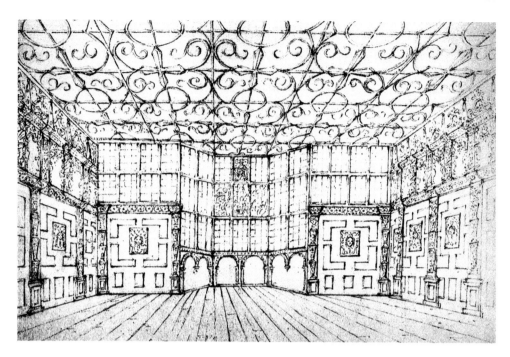

The interior of Bridgeman's amazing house. Note the massive window; a lost treasure.

The building then became the property of William Bird, a silk manufacturer. After his death the house remained empty and semi derelict for many years, was sold in 1820 and shortly afterwards demolished. In 1916 Spectator wrote:

Mr Oldfield was able to recall that in his very juvenile days he used to go through a wide entrance very near to the Banner House, and there, in the rear of the property fronting the street, was a very ancient building, practically falling to pieces, and containing great quantities of old, black oak. The lads of the neighbourhood had the run of the place, a playground, and galloped from room to room, upstairs and down, at their own sweet will; and Mr Oldfield says it seems to him at this distance of time that anyone who wanted wood for any purpose went to this building and fetched it ...

All that survived of this magnificent building was a fine decorated oak mantelpiece which is in the Board Room of Bablake School in Hill Street.

The New House which stood on the corner of Keresley and Sadler roads on the Radford/Keresley boundary was one of the finest houses in the Coventry area. When John Hales of Whitefriar's died, John, his nephew, inherited his estates. In 1586 this second John built the New House on the edge of Whitmore Park. This had previously been the site of a moated hunting lodge belonging to the Bishops of Coventry on the edge of 436 acre, ditched and fenced Whitmore Park. New House with its masses of windows, sat in an elevated position, commanding fine views of the city and spires of Coventry. John let Whitefriar's to Lord Henry Berkley of Caludon Castle.

John Hales died in 1607 and his son, another John, inherited the estate and married Dorothy, daughter of John Croker, Esq., of Gloucestershire; she died in 1623. In 1623 he married Christiana, daughter of John Fullwood of Ford Hall.

Maybe his new wife didn't like New House, for in 1624 John sold it to Sir Richard Burnaby for £1,138; Burnaby sold it onto a certain Cooke, who sold it on in 1656 to Sir Christopher Yelverton of Etton. William Strode, Esquire, rented the building in 1658. He died at the age of thirty-six in 1659, and in 1663 his wife died, and because most of her children had died their rent was neglected and the house was re-let in 1747 to Henry Inge for a payment of 10 guineas and an annual rent of one penny.

Abraham Bohun lived here for some years; he died in 1695, aged seventy-nine. His daughter Judith, married Humphrey Burton who resided with the Bohun's at New House and was coroner of Coventry he died aged thirty-nine. In 1696 Abraham Bohun of New House was succeeded by his son, George Bohun MP, the last male heir of the family died in 1709, aged sixty-five. At his funeral there were twenty-five coaches, a hearse with escutcheons and 200 large candles burned in St Michael's.

In 1716 Gilbert Clarke, who married Susanna, George's eldest daughter, lived at New House. After the Clarkes it had various occupiers till 1778, when it was taken down bit by bit having stood for 192 years. In April the following year an advertisement appeared in the *Coventry Mercury* stating, 'To be Sold at NEW-HOUSE, near this City, the remaining parts of the Materials of the House. Consisting of a large quantity of Timber, Stone, Tiles, Lead, Glass, Iron, etc.'

Afterwards, a smaller house was erected here belonging to the Hopkins family, and afterwards to Mr Smith, who died in 1816. It was sold on to Thomas Ball Troughton who had acquired much of the area. He sold the house on to Abraham Burbery Herbert, who enlarged it, making it a large residence called the Moat House. At this time in the late nineteenth century the original pillars of the principal gateway of New House on the Keresley Road still stood as did the front wall. Moat House was demolished in

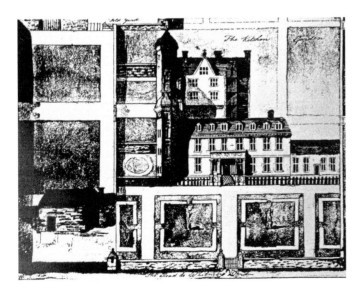

A drawing from the turn of the nineteenth century showing New House and its gardens, another lost Coventry treasure.

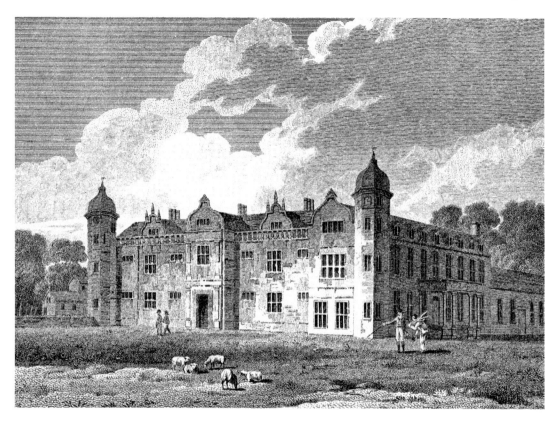

A front view of the New House, its gardens now gone.

the 1920s. Today the only reminder of the New House is the area of grass to the left of where it stood around the Radford Road called New House Green. The problem is, the green bears no name so no-one knows, except you.

In 1852 a large number of lead pilgrims' tokens were found in the Sherbourne behind the Burges. Coventry in the medieval period was a centre of pilgrimage, and pilgrims visited the relics in the priory and the shrine of Our Lady of the Tower built into the city wall. The Pilgrim's Rest was the Guest House of the priory, a half-timber building of considerable size where pilgrims were allowed to stay for three days, leaving on the third day, after dinner. The Guest House may have become redundant after the Dissolution and continued in various hands.

The Priory Guest House alias Pilgrim's Rest stood on the corner of Palmer lane and Ironmonger Row, and in 1819 Mr Joseph Browett with his wife (on a pillion) rode from Northampton to Coventry to take up residence there. The building at that time he described as timbered and had been divided into three properties. The ground floor was used as shops; the first floor was a private house, and the top floor was known as the, 'Lodgers' flat. In 1828 there was a farriery on the ground floor and the lodgers' flat was incorporated into the private house. In order, however, to retain the memory of the old Guest House, a cottage was built at the corner of Palmer Lane and it was this property that was first called 'The Pilgrim's Rest'. The authority of this is one of Browett's daughters, who lived the Guest House before and after the building the Pilgrim's Rest Inn. She said that as late as 1828 her father could see from his back room, down his garden path to where the river Sherbourne ran ...

There was definitely some rebuilding here as later photographs show different buildings. However, decorative stone windows from the old guest house survived in the second inn, for in 1916 they were described, 'In the centre of the first is a man with branches growing out of his head almost in the manner of the antlers stags and on each side are two-footed, winged and human-headed dragons. One head is distinctly that of a woman. The second window portrays a hunting scene with a mounted hunter, pursuing hound and fleeing prey, of whose identity I have some little doubt, though it is probably a stag'. This is especially interesting, for we know that the original inn was decorated with saints and hunting scenes. When the 'modern' Pilgrim's Rest was being demolished in 1936 workmen found remains of an ancient building, mainly at the rear of the property, consisting of timber, daub and wattle and stone tracery. All of which were ripped out. So, although we are told the 'Rest' was demolished in 1820, this was obviously not the case and some of Coventry's ancient guest house did actually survive until 1936.

On 3 November 1916 Coventry City Council accepted a recommendation from the Estates and Finance Committee that the Old Tower Inn, Cook Street be repaired and let.

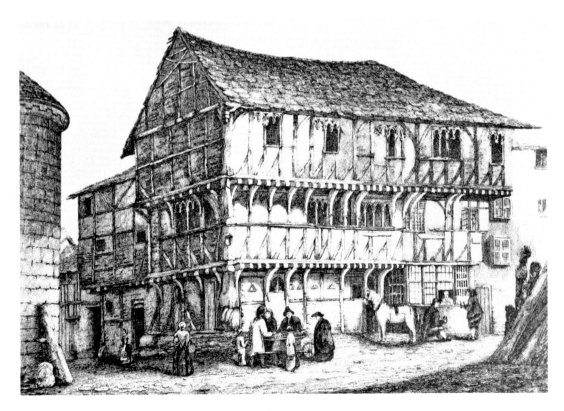

A nineteenth-century engraving of the Pilgrim's Rest.

The old inn was believed to be the gatehouse of Cook Street Tower and it was hoped that the, 'gentlemen concerned will take the character and history of the house into account in the letting, and a tenant will be secured who will bear in mind the antiquarian value of the building'. It was said at the same time.

> You will remember that Messrs. Mitchells and Butlers, the brewers, presented the house to the city. I have been told that the firm refused a very substantial offer for the premises, in the belief that the place should be in the possession of the city, and the remarks which were made at the Council meeting when the gift was accepted illustrated the spirit in which it was received.

The building was inspected in 1916 and it was written;

> The house is built flush up to the north-west corner of the tower, in fact ... the wall of the house that side is part of the tower itself. In the corner of the room, nearest the gate, is an opening in the stonework giving access to narrow stairway which at some remote period has been blocked up. Apparently this stairway led to a second storey of the tower,

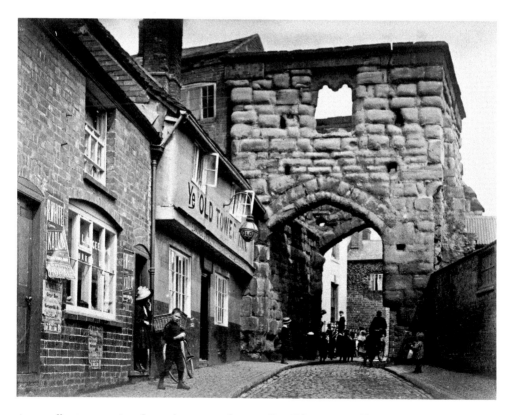

An excellent street view from about 1905 showing 'Ye Old Tower Inn' butted against Cook Street Gate; one of many Coventry pubs destroyed. Recent ones to join the list were the 250-year-old Greyhound and the 160-year-old Rocket. Can we really afford to continue destroying our heritage!

outside the actual structure or in the thickness of the wall. In the second storey of the tower, the north side, a doorway is discernible, which has been something of a puzzle to the antiquaries; this doorway would probably be at the top end of the stairs which started in the room below. If this theory be correct, the room of the inn fronting the street and adjoining the tower may be ... a guard room, perhaps, for the soldier-citizens who kept watch and ward, who opened and closed the gate at the appointed times, and were ready to defend the city from attack. The stone-work by the side of the fire-place in this room, at the height of about four feet, is worn away as if steel had been sharpened upon it. It was suggested that this represents the place where the guards sharpened their knives for domestic purposes. Opinion is, that if this concavity were produced by sharpening processes at all, it would be the sharpening of fighting weapons which did it, just such marks were made in other places by the soldiers sharpening their pikes on the stone-work.

Cook Street gate was presented to the city in 1913 by Sir William Wyley; it was restored in 1918. The fifteenth-century Tower House, formerly the Old Tower Tavern, was given in the same year and was demolished in 1963.

7. Green Men and Hidden Art

All over the country in historic buildings, especially churches, can be found images of the Green Man; a face surrounded by leaves growing out of his mouth. In the Celtic period this God, for it was a God, was known as Esus or Erriapus, the god who looked out of the leaves; a god of nature, the wildwood and protector of nature and the earth mother. This pagan image has been carried through time by the church and can be seen alongside the Virgin Mary. Saint Augustine said that if the old gods were difficult to remove, include them into the Christian faith, and this seems to have happened with the Green Man, who can be found hidden away in buildings all over the country.

Coventry, too, has its fair share of this ancient god of nature. In St Mary's Guildhall in the entrance gate can be seen a fine fourteenth century Green Man with leaves spewing out of his mouth and, strangely, what appears to be a Green Woman (generally an unknown quantity) with branches around her face. On the left of the entrance in the Mercer's Room can be seen a rare crowned green man among numerous rare carvings. Inside the hall at the bottom of the stairs, above the entrance to the old Muniment Room, can be seen another green man dating from 1856. Inside the hall there are two green men, not in the Great Hall as stated in the 1980 guide, that are actually the head of John the Baptist. The two green men, one recut and one original, are in the men's and ladies' toilets upstairs in a private area which occupies the roof space of the old kitchen.

One of the best oak carved green men in the city can be seen hidden under the medieval oak choir stalls in Holy Trinity Church. Two more can be seen, each in oak, placed either end of the Marler's Chapel created by Christopher Marler, once one of the richest merchants in England. Part of the ceiling of the chapel, which is unfinished, is decorated with grapevines and skulls, strangely appropriate considering all the skulls that are stored under this chapel in one of the only existing bone houses in the country. More Green men and grotesques can be found on a medieval door situated at the back of St John's church in Fleet Street.

Some of the other great medieval stone carvings in Coventry also survive in the Mercer's Room in St Mary's Hall. These consist of the crowned green man mentioned before, a maid biting her tongue, a devil with an animal's body, a strange almost Celtic looking shouting longhaired bearded man, another large man's head, and beasts such as griffins and unknown jackal like beasts fighting. On the exterior of the building high up can be seen a fourteenth century woman's head, hardly touched by the elements as it lies on the curve of the building.

The largest number of medieval oak carvings in the city survives in the Great Hall's roof and the Treasury of St Mary's hall, numbering nearly 100. In the hall we see angels playing instruments, Coventry's elephant, hunting griffins eating animals and acting as guardians of the building, unicorns, lions, hinds, elephants, a dragon and

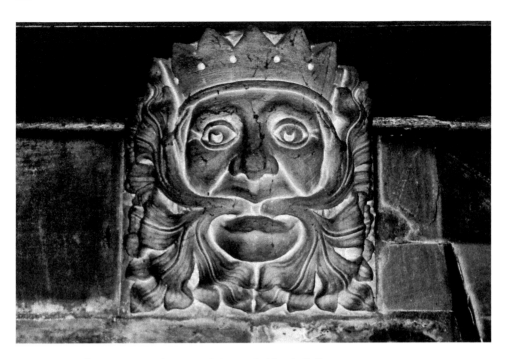

A rare crowned green man in the Mercer's Room, St Mary's Hall.

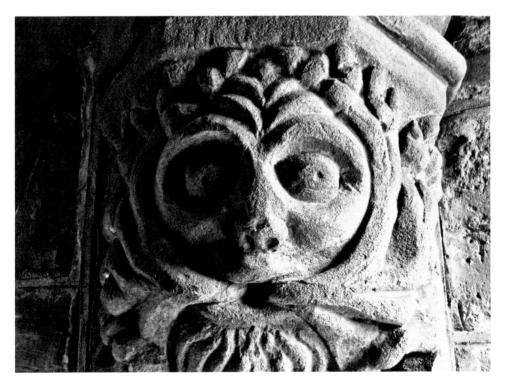

Amazing fourteenth-century green man in the ladies' toilets, St Mary's Hall!

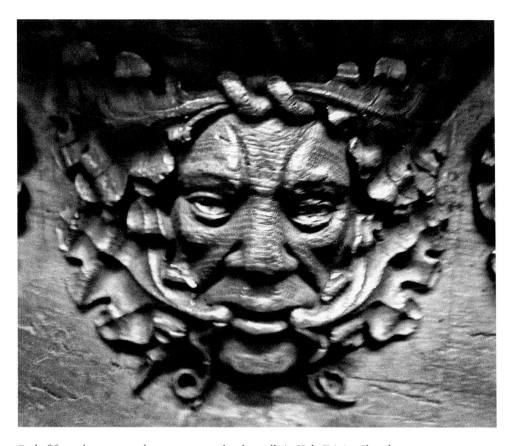

Early fifteenth-century oak green man under the stalls in Holy Trinity Church.

swans of Margaret of Anjou, and dozens of antelopes of Henry VI. In the centre of the ceiling can be seen an eagle on top of a dragon, symbolic of good over evil or Christ defeating the devil. Either side of this can be seen the head of John the Baptist and a head from the reign of Richard II, who died in 1399. Interestingly, this head has a hand, which from the important dais end looks like the man is talking behind his hand (secrecy). But from the north end of the hall the hand appears to be holding one finger up ... the symbol of the Johnnanite, a secret cult who believed that John the Baptist was the real messiah. Johnnanite symbols can be found in the works of da Vinci such as the Last Supper. In the Treasury are survivors of the Pilgrim's Rest, oak carvings of God, St Michael, the Virgin and Child and others. The hall also has one of the most important heavily carved late fourteenth century chairs in England, bearing a remarkable elephant that bears more of a resemblance to a boar.

A fine bearded head by Coventry man John Thornton, who died in the early 1400s and was probably the greatest stained-glass maker ever, can be seen in the Oriel window in St Mary's hall. Other pieces of his work from the old cathedral survive; much is under restoration and hopefully will be displayed in the future. There are also fine panels of Thornton glass displayed in the Undercroft of the new cathedral. Thornton's work at its

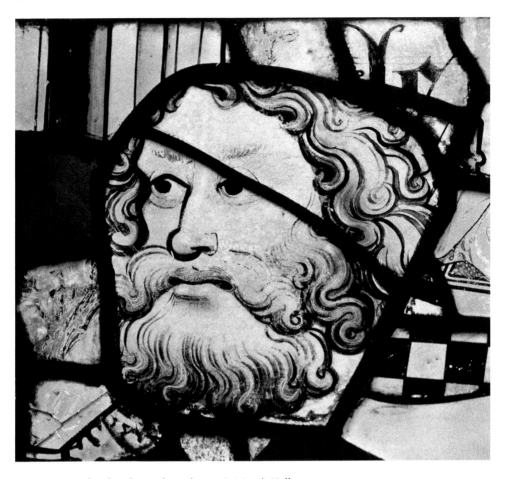

John Thornton head in the oriel window in St Mary's Hall.

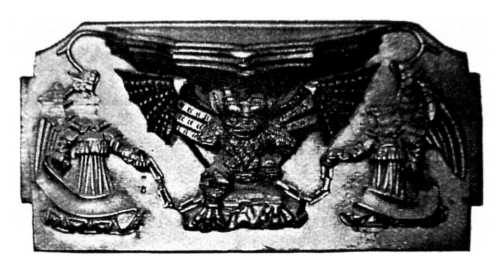

A fine misericord from St Michael, now destroyed, showing the devil in chains!

best was years ahead of his time and his workshop stood in the Burges on the site of the present McDonalds. The oriel windows in St Mary's also contain remains of the only surviving medieval seasonal roundels in the city. One shows a man and wife cutting corn with the legend, 'and with my sickle'. Others show a man flailing corn for the month of September, one shows cutting grapes in October and another shows a man warming his hands before the fire, with flitches of bacon hanging up. This is for November, the blood month, when excess cattle were slaughtered.

Recently, during the archaeological watch in the ruins of St Michael, burned remains of the fine medieval benches were found and show as lumps of black charcoal in the ground of the Lady Chapel; these were once some of the finest medieval benches in Warwickshire. Twelve of these highly decorated benches contained misericords under their seats; carvings showing different themes. One contained the Dance of Death, which shows two gravediggers lowering a shrouded figure into the grave while being blessed. Another depicted the Last Judgement, in which Christ sits on the throne surrounded by angels blowing trumpets while judging the dead. Another had the devil held in chains by two angels, and another shows an angel holding St George's shield with two mermen on either side. One of these benches was even drawn by Pugin for one of his books. Sadly, they were burned on the night of 14 November 1940, three days before they were due to be removed to safety.

Thankfully, the misericords of Holy Trinity survived and can still be seen tucked under the stalls. These include a green man, Wildman and others. Trinity's famous, once hidden, treasure is its massive Doom painting of Christ judging the dead, created probably in the 1430s soon after Coventry suffered an earthquake. The story of the Doom is well known. Hidden through the nineteenth and twentieth centuries by varnish, grime and smoke it was 'rediscovered' a few years ago and brought back to its original glory, and is now one of the finest in Britain.

One of the largest, most seen, pieces of modern art in Coventry stands in the heart of Broadgate; Lady Godiva. Everyone knows the Godiva statue, but does anyone know its secret background? In 1937 William Bassett-Green, a Coventry industrialist, commissioned Sir William Reid-Dick to create this well known sculpture. He began his great work the following year, and soon after, in November 1940, William Bassett-Green left the city after his house was destroyed by bombs and he was nearly killed. The Godiva figure is not as straight forward as one would think; Dick used a number of models for the body. Godiva's arms were of American origin, one arm was modelled from Katherine Killyer, an American writer, the other from Katie Best, also an American. Both were friends of Sir William, and posed for him during the war. Sir William Reid-Dick said in 1949 that he used at least a dozen women. He said, 'Lady Godiva has the hands of one, the feet of another, the shoulders of a third and so on. The long flowing tress of hair was my own idea'. Dick gave the reason for so many models, 'It was wartime when I began the work and models were difficult to find, so I searched for someone who had a good head, another who had the right type of hand, and so on. All sorts of people posed'.

A Miss Beeching posed, but for what he never said. Another who provided the face of Godiva was another friend, Rosanne Snelling. The model for the horse was supplied by Coventry Police. The finished sculpture, costing £20,000 and entitled 'Self-Sacrifice', was cast from two tons of bronze at the Morris-Singer Foundry in 1944. It was then hidden away in the Cotswolds for three years as Dick's studio at the time was thought to be at threat by bombs. It was placed on the pedestal designed by Sir John Burnett and inscribed with lines from Tennyson's poem. It was formally presented to the city in October 1949, and stood in the Garden of Remembrance planted with thousands of tulips given by the Dutch people for the aid they had received in the Great War. Sir William Reid Dick said the statue was 'completely modest and decent and in no way unsuitable for the cathedral precincts'. Perhaps some didn't agree, in fact when she was unveiled many were surprised that Godiva's hair wasn't longer hiding her two most prominent points.

The largest surviving late medieval wall painting survives in the Charterhouse on the London Road. Only the lower section survives, showing Christ bleeding on the cross and the Roman legionnaire, Longinus, and others at his feet. The full painting was split in two when the top half of the once open hall was floored over, creating an upper floor. Charterhouse also has other remarkable wall paintings of a later period. One almost complete wall painting, which is dateable, is in the Mercer's Room in St Mary's hall. It shows the arms of the Mercer's Company, who used the room as a meeting place and chapel, and was painted in the reign of Elizabeth I in 1590. Another particularly interesting painting in the hall, this time on canvas, is in the Old Mayoress' Parlour (Draper's Room). It is believed to date from around 1626, although it looks slightly later

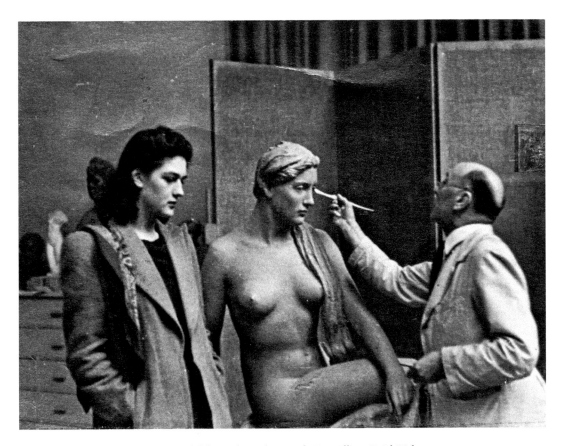

Rosanne Snelling, the face model for Lady Godiva, with Sir William Reid-Dick.

and shows Charles I holding, oddly, the Magna Carta. This is the only painting in the country showing this, and is considered particularly odd considering Charles believed in the ultimate power of kings.

Apart from the well-known remarkable Doom in Trinity, more remarkable paintwork can be seen on the inside of the roof, painted blue with gold stars, and along each cross beam can be seen angels holding implements of Christ's passion. Also, underneath the spire, is a remarkably decoratively painted area ... most of this goes unseen. A symbolic piece of art in the Archdeacon's Court is on the Throgmorton tomb against the north wall. On the face of the tomb can be seen the outline of three brasses, originally the holy trinity, and the Throgmortons with their children. Along the top of the tomb, repeated in decorative squares, a woman's head and a barrel with a mulberry upon it. This tells the name of those buried there. The woman's head is the 'Frow'; an old word once used to describe a woman. This is followed by the mulberry, from old English, 'mor', the heraldic 'mur' or murrey berry seen upon the barrel; the tun ... this is Frowmortun or Throgmorton. Not perfect but a recognisable play on words. The most noted Throgmorton was Sir John Throgmorton, who was the City Recorder when Elizabeth I visited the city in 1565. He gave a fine speech to the queen and was knighted by her.

Coventry has a surprising amount of unnoticed and hidden art, but like all books on Coventry, this one hasn't got enough pages, so that's all I can manage; till next time.

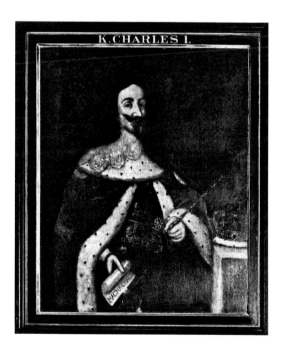

King Charles I as he appears in St Mary's Hall, strangely the only portrait in the nation showing him holding the Magna Carta. Hardly what you expect of someone who believed in the ultimate power of kings!

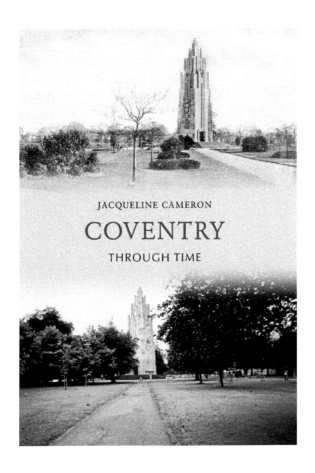

Also Available from Amberley Publishing

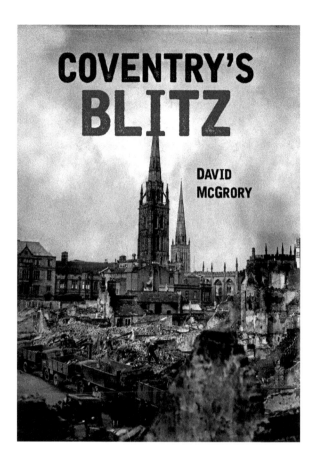

This fascinating selection of photographs traces the effects of the
Second World War on Coventry.

Paperback
180 illustrations
128 pages
978-1-4456-4999-3

Available 2014 from all good bookshops or to order direct
please call **01453-847-800**
www.amberley-books.com